A BEAT FROM
THE HEART
TO THE HEART
OF POWER

A BEAT FROM THE HEART TO THE HEART OF POWER

PHYLLIS SIGSWORTH Q.P.M.

With
DAVID HARNBY

Foreword by Rt Hon
THERESA MAY MP

First published in 2020

ISBN 978-1-913532-03-1

Also available as an ebook
ISBN 978-1-913532-04-8

Typeset by seagulls.net
Cover design by Alice Moore
Project management by whitefox
Printed and bound by Clays

Foreword to Phyllis Sigsworth's book.

In a world where we have seen women become Commissioner of the Metropolitan Police, Director General of the National Crime Agency and Head of the National Police Chiefs Council, it is easy to forget the struggle of the women police officers who went before, who blazed the trail and who in the early days were more often than not accepted under sufferance rather than welcomed. In this book Phyllis Sigsworth brings home the barriers faced by women in the police force, but also the difference that women were able to make to police forces and to the job of policing. She charts her course from humble police station clerk to the then top job for a woman police officer – Assistant to the Chief Inspector of Constabulary. It is a fascinating record of social change but also the heart-warming story of someone who never allowed the prejudices of the day to stop her from doing what she believed in and serving the public.

What is particularly interesting is the way in which she shows how women were able to bring a different approach to policing and recognise what has now become more widely accepted, namely that policing demands toughness and rigour but also thoughtfulness and consideration. This is about more than policing it is about the wider impact that women police officers had and have on society.

It is also the story of someone who has dedicated their life to improving her local community, whether through her role in the police or her many years of community volunteering after her retirement. It is in this latter context that I first met Phyllis, dynamic, enthusiastic keen to get things done but always thoughtful and caring. I immediately saw her as formidable and someone who would brook no nonsense, but it was clear that her driving force was care for others and that she was able to bring considerable experience from her working life in the police to benefit many.

Today we take women police officers for granted. But they have only been able to achieve because women like Phyllis put themselves forward, overcame the barriers, dealt with the prejudice and showed the way.

To Phyllis and the others who went before we say thank you.

ACKNOWLEDGEMENTS

I would like to thank David Harnby for writing this account of my memories. Without his input and fervour, I would not have produced this book.

Any proceeds from the book's sale, after some publication costs, will be donated to DASH (Domestic Abuse Stops Here), a charity in East Berkshire which supports victims of domestic abuse. This is an issue which I dealt with throughout my career and I hope in some small way I can continue to help those victims who have suffered or who are still suffering.

Phyllis Sigsworth

ABOUT THE AUTHOR

David Harnby worked for 33 years at an international company whose UK operation was based in Maidenhead. He joined Seiko UK Ltd as a graduate from Portsmouth in the junior role of Sales Administrator and finished his career as a Senior Manager and UK Director of the Company. David is currently enjoying a partial early retirement whilst also working part-time in a consulting capacity for a local business.

Having grown up in Middlesbrough in the north-east heartland of England and having been involved in three publications relating to Middlesbrough Football Club, he has huge affection for this part of the country where Phyllis spent much of her career.

His father, Gordon "worked" alongside Phyllis in the early 1980s helping at St Luke's Church, until his untimely death in 1984. Since that time Phyllis and his mother, Joan have become great friends enjoying regular tea and cake sessions and annual holidays away together! As a family friend, David encouraged Phyllis to have her career highlights made into print and was thrilled when she came to that conclusion herself and asked him to help with collating and writing her memoirs.

INTRODUCTION

A BEAT FROM
THE HEART

On 27th January 1950, my life changed in ways I could not have imagined at the time. On this day I was appointed as Policewoman Constable in the North Riding of Yorkshire. At first glance, there may seem nothing extraordinary about that, but looking back nearly 70 years as I write these memoirs, it was a completely different world back then.

Women working in the police force only a few short years after the end of the Second World War were something of a rarity, with strict guidelines in place discriminating against the widespread introduction of women into the forces. Women were simply not allowed to join the police service before the age of 22 and being unmarried was an absolute prerequisite.

At that time, I was working as a civilian clerk in the historic town of Thirsk, in the heart of the North Riding of Yorkshire and I had my heart set on joining the police force. I was aware of the conditions so was thrilled when I discovered, through researching the police regulations, that an exception could be made to join the force at the tender age of 20, providing the Chief Constable of the local force applied to the Home Office on your behalf to request permission. That's all I needed to know, and I approached the man to whom I am eternally grateful, Chief Constable Lieutenant-Colonel Chaytor. He made the request and, ultimately, I was accepted into the police force, shortly after I had reached my 20th birthday.

Instantly I had become one of the youngest policewomen in the country and felt so proud. I had reached the first of my ambitions, but little did I know then of the twists and turns my life would take as I journeyed with the provincial police forces (across England and Wales, excluding London) throughout the next three decades.

Thirty years for this WPC flew by and my retirement in 1979, from within the walls of the Home Office, enabled me to look back on that dramatic moment in my life and my career in the force. My career flourished from patrolling the beat of a small Yorkshire town as one of their local bobbies, to becoming Assistant to the Chief Inspector of the Constabulary, the highest position any woman could achieve as a senior police officer in the provinces at that time.

Working in a largely male-dominated world for those 30 years, I was able to experience at first-hand seismic changes both in attitudes towards women police officers and to women in society in general. At the same time, I could see how every police force operated in the way their own specific region needed to be policed.

I record these memoirs, over 40 years on from my retirement, simply because with much reflection I didn't want my experiences to go unnoticed: because they help shed light on the hugely important role that women police officers from across the country played in society, especially during the 1960s and 70s. I hope my story helps illustrate the massive contribution female officers played in the police service.

CHAPTER 1

WOMEN IN THE POLICE FORCE

As a young girl growing up in North Yorkshire, I never really had any aspirations to be a police officer. The truth was that women police officers were still almost unheard of and rarely seen on the streets of Thirsk where I was living, so for me the profession didn't really exist! That's not to say the police force didn't run in the family. My mother had two uncles who were both in the Durham police force and they were joined later by one of her cousins. Male of course!

My formative years in education were at Easingwold and Thirsk Grammar Schools, where I studied from 1940 to 1945 – throughout the Second World War. From there, armed with School Certificates in seven subjects, I went to the Commercial School in York and obtained Certificates for Shorthand, Typewriting, Bookkeeping and Commercial Arithmetic. However, my passion for wanting to join the police started after I had left formal education and joined a Police Training Centre as a shorthand typist in August 1946. During this period I learned that there were roles for women to work in the police force. Once I knew that was a feasible option, it became my obsession!

There were prerequisites of course. I had to be 22 and unmarried. Well, as a single girl and no long-term Romeo in sight, the second of these conditions was no problem, but the overriding obstacle was that I was still only 17. I had to be patient, and thorough. In July 1948 I left the Police Training Centre to become a clerk at the North Riding Constabulary. I was getting closer. Through a little investigative work, I had established that there was another way of getting into the force two years earlier than advertised – at the more tender age of 20 – so that became my new goal. I simply needed the Chief Constable of the North Riding Constabulary to recommend me to the Home Office.

My focus was clear. With the eagerness of youth and being of tenacious spirit, once I found that an opportunity existed, I took charge. My persistence paid off and to my great relief I was accepted and having turned 20 on 3rd November 1949, all I needed was a vacancy at the station! There wasn't one. Thankfully, I only had to wait a couple of months before things changed.

Before looking ahead to my career in the police force, I think it is important to look back at how a position in the force was able to become a realistic opportunity for me – a woman – in the first place. I really want to put things into perspective by looking briefly at the evolution of the police force in England

and the involvement that women had in helping maintain law and order in the decades which preceded my contribution.

Prior to 1829 and Sir Robert Peel's Metropolitan Police Act there was no paid police force as we know it today and parish constables appointed by residents in a community carried out this duty. However, to begin with I'd like to go back even further – nearly three centuries.

It was fascinating to read in George Howard's book, *Guardians of the Queen's Peace* about the first record I had found of any woman law enforcement officer. In 1695 reference was made to a woman holding the reins of office but aided by a man in order to provide 'that sufficient degree of bodily strength'. The *Quarterly Sessions of the annals of Thirsk (Yorkshire)* records that on 2nd April 1695, 'Ann Sigsworth and her son be discharged from the office of Constable of the town of Great Smeaton and the inhabitants to pay unto the said Ann Sigsworth such money as she shall fairly make appear she hath disbursed for the said town.'

Is this a curious and happy coincidence for me? The name of the woman who held that office of Parish Constable in the parish of Great Smeaton in North Yorkshire – Ann Sigsworth – she may well have been a very old relation of mine. I would love to believe that this Ms Sigsworth was one of my ancestors and indeed it may be true, but without compelling evidence to confirm that fact, the case remains open... As a Yorkshire lass myself, from Thirsk, the chances that my name traces back to another Sigsworth from Yorkshire must be quite high, but my research of the parish archives in Northallerton has not yet uncovered that elusive connection. For me it would provide some completeness, knowing that I was able to continue what my ancestor had started, all those years ago.

In 1829 Home Secretary Sir Robert Peel introduced the first full-time, professional, and centrally organised police force in the Greater London area. This was really the start of a campaign to improve public order across society in metropolitan areas; however, its reform was relatively slow at the time, and there was an initial distrust of the police at many levels.

By the mid-1840s, with new forces emerging all over the country and without any central office, there was not surprisingly great disparity in the form of policing between different areas of the country, with no single official style of policing in place. Many boroughs had appointed parish constables, who were often part-time, poorly paid or sometimes even unpaid, so these posts tended to attract a low calibre of persons, who were not prepared to risk themselves to arrest anyone.

By 1855 there were still only 12,000 policemen in England and Wales, even though the Metropolitan force in London had proved effective in reducing crime and increasing detection of crime. The County Borough Police Act, 1856 obliged the whole country to set up police forces, which for the first time were subject to government control and effectively saw the start of the modern police service in England and Wales. Overall, 239 forces were established, all exclusively staffed by men throughout the remainder of the 19th century. However, whilst the Home Office was theoretically the head of the British police forces with concrete power over the Metropolitan Police, its role in a broader capacity was simply as advisor to the provincial forces, with decisions left in the hands of the local authorities.

With structured police forces now in place and regulated, the relations between the police and the public was close and cordial and this was greatly helped by the absence of any specialised social service agencies. The police ran the fire brigade and ambulances, there were no juvenile courts and the police were able to retain the role of the citizen's friend and helper. A mild system of policing was maintained. The police were not professional in any recognised sense of the term today, but they acted with good humour and kindliness and probably got away with a great deal without any special powers of professionalism.

The one consistent theme in all the provincial forces across England and Wales during this period was the complete absence of women in the profession. Indeed, at the end of the Victorian era and in the first half of the 20th century, there were numerous obstacles which prevented official recognition of policewomen in Britain. There was a widespread male misconception that women could not be trusted as police officers, especially in cases where young men were concerned; it was believed they would be too easily swayed by emotion and would be more likely to fall in love with the man they had been sent to watch!

The 1890s have records of women being included in the forces as 'matrons', who were largely tasked with guarding women and children, and were often the wives or relatives of the police officers. It was only in the years prior to the First World War that there became growing public awareness that there were no female constables, even though there were often women held as prisoners in police custody. This led to campaigning to highlight the issue and from 1911, there were several unofficial street patrols by women in an effort to maintain public morality and decency. With the advent of the War, and with the country deprived of many able-bodied men, women began organising voluntary police patrols to help assist women during the ensuing turmoil. The Women's Police Service, made up of volunteers, was founded in 1914.

By the end of the First World War many cities around the country had women's police voluntary controls in situ, who helped patrol the streets to watch over women and children whose plight may have led them to crime. There were even a couple of incidents of women getting appointed as police officers and given the full powers of arrest in cases where women were involved. This occurred in the provinces – key cities, like Bristol, Hull, Southampton and Liverpool – where they tried to reduce the number of prostitutes, who had been attracted there by the local naval bases.

The War had united the country with women proving their value in undertaking police duties which had hitherto been exclusively performed by men. The First World War heralded many changes in society at that time and in many respects contributed to a desire to maintain and even develop women's role in the police. The work undertaken by women in the factories and in the cities had lain to rest the idea that the workplace was an inherently masculine domain, whilst the rebuilding of cities and the appearance of new leisure venues like cafés and teashops lent themselves to a female clientele. These big provincial cities represented both opportunities and threats to women, and many argued these needed to be policed gender - specifically, by women police.

With the First World War shining a torch on the role of women, those aged 30 and above were enfranchised for the first time as the guns stopped in 1918. In the same year, Parliament passed the Sex Disqualification (Removal) Act. This opened the door for women to become lawyers, vets, civil servants – and police officers. A year later, on the orders of the Home Secretary, the first female police officers joined the Metropolitan Police to patrol the streets of London.

But there was still only a grudging acceptance of – if not visible hostility towards – the contribution of these 'lady policemen'. The commissioner of the Met, Sir Neil Macready, for example, made it abundantly clear that he did not want to be in command of 'vinegary spinsters' or 'blighted middle-aged fanatics'! Moving to the provincial forces, the role of the female officers was often shaped by the views and possible prejudices of the local chief constables.

Back in the 1920s, the role of women officers on patrol was closely monitored. They were only allowed to patrol in pairs and had to be followed by two hefty policemen, who could quickly come to their aid if needed.

Just as height qualifications existed for their male counter-parts, new female recruits had to be at least five feet four inches tall, but they also faced gender-specific barriers. Those with young children were not allowed to serve. Women could not be sworn in as constables. And while they were provided with pay and conditions alongside male officers, women were not given any pension rights.

As Britain moved into the 1920s, there was a widespread perception that the contribution of women was not 'proper police work'. Instead it was akin to welfare, more associated with what we know as social work than mainstream policing. Indeed, female police officers around the country were all too frequently deployed on cases involving women and children.

The decade saw mixed messages coming out of the corridors of power. The Baird Committee concluded that women had more than proved their value in undertaking police duties, which had previously been in the exclusive preserve of men. But this was also a decade of extreme hardship as Britain recovered from the cost of war. As a money-saving exercise, the Home Secretary proposed to dissolve the women's section of the Met, citing the old argument that their work was welfare related.

Incredible by today's standards of course, but there was also a belief that any benefit from employing women was solely linked to a role in 'saving growing girls from temptation'. Concern had been expressed in some quarters of the supposed link between sexual immorality and the number of offences being committed, which had been accentuated following the enhanced role of women in the First World War and their subsequent emancipation.

Women police officers continued to focus predominantly on cases involving women and children, although their responsibilities did widen to include patrol work in large open spaces and parkland, hospital duty and escorting juvenile and female prisoners. Regulations had been issued by the Home Office that clarified the position of policewomen, but forces were still under no obligation to recruit them.

As the 1930s dawned, there was still a commonly held belief that police work was men's work and women in uniform were unashamedly compromising their femininity. If evidence was needed which articulated this attitude and highlighted the indifference of both the Home Office and chief constables towards the value of policewomen, it was the publication of the National Service Handbook, which showed there were no plans for enrolling women as special constables.

But as war once again came onto the horizon, the Women's Auxiliary Police Corps was established in August 1939. Women aged between 18 and 55 were eligible to join, and during the early years of the Second World War, they could perform limited clerical, telephone, and catering police duties. Those who were able to also drove and maintained police vehicles.

The first half of the 20th century had seen some major advancements in the way women were viewed by society and especially in the workplace, but there remained an undercurrent of unease and unwillingness for women to be fully accepted within the Home Office as police officers. One initiative which later became of special interest to me was the Government Committee which had been set up in 1926 to look at the role of women in the police force. One of its recommendations was that a woman should be appointed on a national level, to join the staff of the Police Inspectorate.

As it happens, this did not materialise until after the end of the Second World War when, in 1947, Miss Barbara Denis de Vitré was promoted to the national role of Assistant HM Inspector with special responsibilities for women serving in the police forces within the provinces (which excluded the Metropolitan Police). She was ably assisted by a Staff Officer, Miss Hill, and together they visited all the forces across England and Wales, inspecting women officers and advising the respective chief constable on any matters regarding women in the police.

Miss de Vitré was the most senior-ranking woman police officer in Britain. Little did I know back in 1950 when I joined the force that I would step into her shoes some 28 years later. Miss de Vitré was the first to reach this position, and on my ultimate retirement in 1979, I became the last. The women's section subsequently ceased and separate women's inspections and reports ended. These were integrated into the general inspections across the force, of both policemen and policewomen.

That initial role played by Miss de Vitré in the Inspectorate was hugely important to the changing duties performed by female police officers across the country. Her influences were critical to my own career development and my story begins shortly after she had been initiated into her national position.

I hope that I can recall and retell my own real-life experiences which help illustrate the role in the police force experienced by me – a woman – and ultimately dispel the idea that a women police officer's only role was to look after women and children. I also hope that I am able to show very clearly how women were able to progress through the 1950s, 60s and 70s in what was a very male-dominated occupation.

CHAPTER 2

CIVILIAN LIFE
A PRELUDE TO JOINING
THE POLICE FORCE

I attended Grammar Schools in Easingwold and Thirsk, then Commercial School in York, leaving full time education in July 1946. Like many other young adults at that age, I didn't know for sure where my life was heading or what sort of career I was about to embark upon.

I had an aptitude for shorthand and typing, but as I came to appreciate many times over, a formal schooling education only helps to a point. The real learning comes from real-life experiences in the real world.

Quite where my schooling to date was going to lead me remained something of an enigma, but looking back to that period, it's fair to say that the police force as such had not really crossed my mind as a potential career path. Yet, it's possible that there may have been something in my subconscious that steered me towards the joining staff at the No. 2 District Police Training Centre at Easingwold.

There had been police influences during my childhood as my mother's two uncles had both worked in the Durham Constabulary and had both retired after being promoted to the position of Inspector. My mother used to tell me that as a teenager, she was sent to help her uncle's family whenever a new baby came on the scene and whilst she was there, she was also asked to help with the feeding of prisoners in custody at the police station. At that time, when people were kept in cells, the wife of the officer in charge at the station had to take responsibility for feeding them and supervising them when necessary.

I should add at this point that during this period a policeman's wife was not allowed to take employment on her own behalf. This was very much contrary to other working-class groups, but there remained fear within early 20th-century society that a policeman's working wife might be tempted to use influence or be put under pressure because of the nature of her husband's job. Police officers were meant to appear as members of the 'respectable working class', despite their relatively low wages at the time, and since the wives of such men did not work, the same was made true for police officers. Imagine the furore if that was a condition of work in today's world.

I joined the Police Training Centre in August 1946 and started work as a shorthand typist for the police staff, including the training instructors. From the start I very much felt part of the team, even though I was employed as a civilian, working within a structured police unit.

Accommodation was provided, so I lived at the Training Centre itself alongside the instructors, the Commandant and all the other staff in the main house, called Hawkhills. The recruits lived in the adjoining Centre premises. We all ate together in the rather palatial rooms of that wonderful old house, so it was an excellent way of integrating with the team. I hold such fond memories of that period, enjoying the camaraderie of my 'new family', whilst being able to absorb so much information about the role of the police and their service to the community.

In the main house there was a games room where I spent many an evening becoming a dab hand at table tennis and beating most of my rivals into submission! There was also a separate bar room, where despite being the 'baby' of the group by quite a few years and clearly under drinking age, I was granted permission to visit and join in the evening banter with my older colleagues. As a glass of beer or wine was off the menu, it must have been here that I developed my long-term addiction to the delights and perils of Vimto, which was my new-found evening tipple!

I was very much at home at Hawkhills and I had always imagined that my mother would have given it the thumbs up as a suitable home from home. I had never asked for her approval because it was ultimately my decision to leave home and move on, following my own path to the next stage of my life. However, it was somewhat reassuring when I found out that my mother and grandfather had, unbeknown to me, previously visited the premises and chatted with the Commandant to make sure in their own minds that it was a suitable place for me to move away from home to live and work. It was comforting to know that I had the support of my family, even if I had found out retrospectively!

I had always valued the opinion of my mother and grandfather, who really had taken on the role of my own father, after my dad had died when I was only seven. Grandad owned a farm – College Farm at Byland Abbey – and we moved there shortly after my mother became widowed. He was a strict disciplinarian and because of this I learned right from wrong very quickly and at a young age. Perhaps this helped propel me into a world of wanting to help society rebalance the wrongs with justice and serving the community.

Those formative years growing up on a farm were very memorable, living in the countryside and next to the ruins of Byland Abbey. I distinctly recall that even though the Farm and the Abbey were situated on their own individual land, both buildings were connected by a secret underground tunnel, which used to set my imagination running wild as to why it had been used in days gone by. I never fully understood the connection, but it was a thrill to know that many a secret may have lain hidden within my grandfather's old farm.

I attended the junior school in Coxwold and spent many a happy hour in the company of two retired school teachers who ran the Sunday School in the local village of Wass, taking walks across the moors, with them helping, almost subconsciously, my education across a whole variety of subjects. Their teachings clearly worked because I was able to take my eleven plus certificate early, at the age of ten, which in turn helped me take my "O" levels at the age of 14, at least a year younger than many of my friends.

Around this time my Grandfather sold his farm and we all moved to Thirsk where I carried on with further education until I joined the Commercial School in York. This required a daily journey by train from Thirsk to York, which helped even further in building my own independence and not having to rely on others to help me make things happen.

Because I was fortunate enough to take and pass my certificates early, it meant that I was effectively a year ahead of my peers when I ultimately left college and started my first job at the Training Centre. Whilst it was not my original intention for my first job to quickly develop into a potential career path, because I was working in such proximity to the training centre facilities, I was seeing at first hand every day how the new recruits were able to progress and ready themselves for joining the police force.

This really opened my eyes, enabling me to see on a daily basis the new recruits who attended the Training Centre, and the type of training they had to undertake. I had yet to see any women involved in training and it became apparent very quickly that there were absolutely no training facilities for women at Easingwold. I learned that any training for female recruits at that time took place at two different centres in the provinces – at Bruche and at Mill Meece. Nevertheless, I wondered why there were so few new female recruits choosing the police force as their career.

I was aware that women were employed as constables but so rarely were they visible to the general public. As I had found during my own childhood, it was unusual to see a female officer on the beat. I learned very quickly that there were only 12 women uniformed officers serving in the North Riding, spread over the whole county, working in different divisions; whilst across England and Wales, each provincial force was restricted to having no more than 5% women officers in their total establishment.

From this point I started questioning why there was little career structure for women in the police force; it just didn't seem right to me. The simple answer is because there were so few women employed in the police force in the first place, so establishing a career structure was entirely superfluous at that time. It caused me to ponder further. Why shouldn't a female officer carry out the same duties as her male counterpart and why were there so many restrictions in place to join the police in the first place? It didn't seem entirely fair and I'm sure this inequality helped fuel my ambitions to show that I could achieve as well as anyone else – man or woman.

My interest in the police as a career grew and I began questioning things with increased fervency as I took it upon myself to find out more about the regulations and procedures in place. My ambitions were gaining momentum.

During my time at Easingwold one of the instructors gave me the quote from *Guardian of the Queen's Peace*, which I mentioned earlier, and had brought to my attention the role of Ann Sigsworth as the first documented record of a woman working in any type of law and order capacity. Maybe this connection by name, however tenuous it may or may not have been, served to inspire me, at the same time as I was gradually gaining further insights into law. The surroundings, the insights, the everyday living within the 'police world' were energising me. My desire to join the police force intensified, my interest in the law was fired up, and I became much more focused on establishing how I could find a way into my intended new profession.

Things came to a head when the centre at Easingwold closed and the Police Training Centre moved to Plawsworth in County Durham. Hawkshill reverted to the Civil Defence HQ, which had previously occupied the house during the Second World War. I had the opportunity to remain at Easingwold and join the staff of the Civil Defence, as secretary to the Commandant, but this isn't what I had in mind. When the Assistant Chief Constable of North Riding, John E. S. Brown asked me what I wanted to do, I was able to reply with real conviction, after all I had experienced at the Training Centre, that I most definitely wanted to become a policewoman. There was one small obstacle – the age of entry for women into the force was 22 and I was a mere 18 years old. My early schooling success had effectively kept me one year further back from joining the police force. Or so I thought…

Four years seemed a long way away, but I was given the opportunity of an administrative job at Northallerton, Headquarters of the North Riding Constabulary, which was a step closer than being a secretary at the Civil Defence HQ.

The opportunity arose at the Police HQ because I had got to know the police officers whilst at Training Centre and I'd like to think that I had impressed them with my positive attitude, willingness to learn and eagerness to get involved.

To my good fortune, early into my service at Northallerton, the only male cadet at Thirsk Station left his post to do national service. I say male cadet in order to distinguish from female cadets, but the fact is that there were no female cadets in the force, nor indeed anywhere in the country! I couldn't understand why this was the case, so I asked if I could take his place. Looking back, making this request highlighted again, that there were gender inequalities, with barriers in place preventing an easy path for women to follow and make progress.

This was not only common in the police force but across society in general, irrespective of profession and perhaps not too surprising given that this was the late 1940s, only a few years after the massive upheaval and turbulence caused by the Second World War. Society would need time to reflect, readjust and make progress. Nevertheless, I was anxious and ambitious, and I wanted change more quickly. I just couldn't accept that I was not regarded as being capable of doing the same work – or better work – than a male colleague. I was very rational in my approach as I have always believed that talking with genuine belief and good sense will prevail and help break down communication barriers. It was eventually agreed by the Standing Joint Committee that I could work at the office in Thirsk, replacing the cadet, but with the title of clerk. I had won the battle, so I didn't argue about the title!

As clerk at the police station in Thirsk, I was dealing with various incidents which were brought to the front desk, so I could then pass them on to the officer in charge at the station to proceed with any further necessary investigative procedures. With three of us working in the station it was quite rare for me to be left on my own to deal with any issues, because quite simply the principle was that I should never be left on my own! However, on one occasion, with both my colleagues out on important police duties, I was left alone. Back in those days, if there was a fire, the siren had to be sounded at the police station to call out the firemen.

I'd always wanted to do that – sound the siren – and now I had the opportunity! A call had come to the station saying there was a fire locally, so as the only person at the station I had to take responsibility, and action. With great excitement I sounded the siren and whenever the phone rang asking of the whereabouts of the fire, I felt fully in control and advised everybody accordingly. Then my inspector returned and asked me if I had told everyone where the fire was. I proudly said 'yes', as I was pleased to have carried out all the necessary instructions as if I had been a police constable. I felt a bit deflated when rather than getting praised for my quick and efficient work, I was told emphatically that I should never tell the press or others anything to do with police conduct. The main sentiment of that 'ticking off', of keeping police matters very close to my chest, stayed with me for many years!

The time before I could apply to join the force would not pass by quickly enough for me and my ambitions solidified as the weeks went by. I quickly realised that I was not only desperate to join the police force but I was determined to progress within the service and be promoted to the level of Inspector by the time my retirement came into effect all those years into the future. By doing so, I would then be on a par with my two great uncles who themselves had achieved this rank by the time they had both retired from the force. Little did I know back then that my career ambition was to be reached by the age of 30, at least 20 years before my actual retirement!

I have always regarded myself as a 'bit of a nosy parker', which is another way of saying that I had natural investigative instinct and left no stone unturned in my pursuit of the truth! This helped me bring forward my aspirations to join the police force. I was beginning to think that I would never be old enough to become a policewoman: 22 sounded a long way off as an 18-year-old. However, I was fortunate to have access to police regulations and through my own inquisitiveness, I discovered that a woman could join the force prior to the age of 22, and in fact could become a constable at the age of 20, providing the chief constable considered her to be a special case and applied to the Home Office for permission on her behalf.

That was all I needed to know, and I now had the bit between my teeth. My then Chief Constable, Lieutenant-Colonel Chaytor quickly learned of my enthusiasm to join the force. In fact, I had known him from a young age, and he had seen me grow up over the years and had witnessed my gradually increasing appetite for wanting the police to become my career of choice. I subsequently approached him, quoting the regulation and he made an application to the Home Office for me to be considered as a recruit. Things were in motion and it was with great excitement and anticipation that the application was approved, and it was ultimately confirmed that I could be appointed into the police force on the date of my 20th birthday, 3rd November 1949. My wish had been granted and I was very relieved… and very happy!

However, my natural enthusiasm was tempered somewhat with several anxious moments as my 20th birthday approached, since there were simply no vacancies in the North Riding forces. This meant that virtually every day in the weeks leading up to 3rd November, a phone call was made by me to HQ to check on the latest news and ask if anyone had resigned and a vacancy had become available.

Looking back, I could feel a bit sorry for the Admin Office, having to put up with my constant attention, but through it all, the office will have seen my determination, my tenacity and my absolute desire to fulfil my ambition. These character traits would ultimately help serve me through the challenges I would face over the next 30 years and beyond.

I had already passed my medical and been issued with my uniform (just to keep me quiet for a while I think), all in readiness for 'the big day', which sadly didn't materialise immediately. I'm pleased to say, as things turned out, I didn't have to wait too much longer, and I was eventually sworn in as a Police Constable on the 27th January 1950. My first ambition had been fulfilled. I was delighted and incredibly proud.

Two days later, I was on my way to Police Training Centre…

CHAPTER 3

TRAINING CENTRE
THE PATH TO MY NEW CAREER

I was awash with different emotions as I stood on the platform at Thirsk railway station on that momentous Sunday morning. Trepidation, excitement, apprehension, a few nerves perhaps but mainly excitement… I was about to embark on a short journey by train which, unknown to me at the time, would propel me on a much longer life-changing journey into my new career in the police force.

Sundays have always held a special place for me – a day to reflect, rejoice and connect with my faith. A special day to have a quiet word with God in the hope of righting all the wrongs in this world; and, perhaps a private moment to ask for His advice to help guide me on my own life's choices. I'm sure looking back to that Sunday, 29th January 1950, that I had several conversations with Him, seeking reassurances that I was doing the right thing in getting embedded into a predominantly male-orientated sector, whilst endeavouring to make a difference in my own way, by looking forward to protecting and serving the community.

Attending Police Training Centre was mandatory for all new police recruits from the provincial forces in England and Wales, at one of several regional training centres. My 'home' for the next 13 weeks was the relatively new centre for police training at Bruche, near Warrington, which had opened only a few years earlier. In its previous life, the training centre had been an old RAF centre with wooden army huts and communal washrooms, but had been subsequently taken over by the police as a training centre designed to take raw recruits and mould them into police officers who would serve and protect our communities. Over the next 60 or so years, this centre was to train many thousands of officers until its eventual closure in May 2006. I can look back now and imagine with a wry smile, the blood, sweat and tears, wrung from all the 'old' new recruits put through their wide and varied drill routines, all to make our society a safer and happier place to live.

Very quickly, and for the first time in my early association with the police, I found an area of equality between male and female officers. It became very clear that gender was not considered in any way when it came to the training programme – both men and women received the same instruction. We did the same training, went on to perform the same job, but there, equality ended: women only received 90% of the men's pay! I did wonder about that but didn't dwell on it for too long. After all, my motivations were less about trying to make as much money as I could, than taking pride in doing a job to the best of my ability and to make a difference.

When I joined the School at Bruche, there were very few women officers in my syndicate – two of us in fact, alongside 23 male officers. We had all taken our Oath of Allegiance and had been sworn in as new recruits to the profession, before we set out on our 13 weeks of intensive training, in preparation for us to cope with any challenge or offence which would face us in the days, weeks and years ahead. These weeks of intensive training would be followed with two-week refresher courses after one year and then again after the second year – during the probationary period and before confirmation of being appointed as a constable. I didn't really appreciate at the time that those basic grounding lessons learned over a three-month period would help provide me with the necessary learnings, in conjunction with my own developing character traits, to reach the top of my profession some 30 years later.

There was a lot expected from everyone. The training itself included lectures and seminars covering all aspects of police work – traffic control, criminal law, first aid, lifesaving and drill – whilst we were also expected to absorb a working knowledge of broader aspects of the law, literally cramming police studies of all kinds into a 13-week window of opportunity. All the instructors were male and there was no favour shown during any of the exercises; each of us had to prove ourselves on merit, which I was more than happy to go along with.

The other woman recruit and I had joined the service from the position of Civilian Clerks. Not surprisingly (given the close proximity to the end of the Second World War) the majority of the male officers had come from a military background and were therefore well-rehearsed in the exercise which quickly became my bête noir: the drill! My female colleague and I had a lot in common and we often studied together. Sad to say, we were both humiliated on the parade ground!

I'd never received any instruction in drill prior to the training exercises and it soon became pretty obvious to everyone that I couldn't march… and truth beknown I still can't! So, I was always filled with trepidation and fear whenever the barking voice of the drill sergeant was close by. I was a thorn in his side! I was one of those 'different' people that work the wrong leg with the wrong arm and often at the wrong time! That drill sergeant, whose name I'm rather pleased to say I have forgotten, was very cruel and he tried long and laboriously to correct my marching, but without much success.

This challenging trait haunted me in the years which followed. When my career progressed and I was a sergeant in Northumberland, we had a centenary parade which required me to lead the parade for the women officers and act as their right marker, so they could follow the march in sequence. Sadly, for me, this march was filmed on a cine-camera and played back to the force later. It clearly showed both male and female officers marching elegantly, but with one exception – a female who waddled out of step, rather than march in line; I hung my head in shame!

Years later when I was the inspecting officer at a cadets' passing out parade in Durham, I noticed that one of my fine young students did not appear on parade but instead was carrying out some mundane duty of parking cars. On asking her why she wasn't on parade with her colleagues, she revealed that she couldn't march! Such was her concern that her very worried parents also caught up with me, scared in case her lack of marching ability would prevent her from being allowed to join or progress in the force. I was able to put their minds completely at rest by carefully explaining my own marching inadequacies and that it had not prevented me from making a good career in the force. As it happened this young cadet went on to become a very good police constable.

My female colleague and I vied throughout the course for first place in the exams and our hard work was very much rewarded. The course was very interesting and informative with studies across the police spectrum. One area in which I received little instruction at the time but mastered later in my own time, was Point Duty. This was a requirement for police officers to control the movement of traffic at junctions. The reason why I had to master this skill in my own time? It takes me back to the time when I was working as a civilian clerk and through the office windows, I would often see officers undergoing training exercises in traffic control. My old Commandant at the time, a lovely gentleman called Norman Lee, used to refer to these policemen undergoing point duty as 'playing silly bees'. Unfortunately, I couldn't get this image out of my mind and I interrupted the class with my giggles. I am embarrassed to say that I was sent out of the class!

Self-defence was an important aspect of training and revolved around the art of judo. It was very useful but with judo it seemed to me that you needed to have your opponent in the right position to be able to perform a move. I often smiled to myself thinking how a villain might react if I was to ask him to keep still for a moment so I could manoeuvre him into a better position to make the right hold and prevent him from moving!

During my career, I rarely had to use any physical force and in my early years I often found that it was my femininity which helped me tackle an arrest, especially if the perpetrator was a man. In a nutshell, you could simply talk to them, almost 'chat them up' in fact and there seemed restraint and respect. By talking civilly to them I always found that they gave me great respect and their attitude changed. Women prisoners – yes – there was often a problem, but with men, to be honest, I never had any problems. I always found that female police officers were able to lower the temperature of situations, perhaps by being simply 'a woman' and not trying to be a 'female man'. Mind you that was in a different age, and society has changed over the years and with it a different attitude towards law officers, male or female.

As I mentioned, there were no female instructors at the training centre, nor any special instruction for the 'specialist' role women officers would have to undertake on their return to their forces. This only really became apparent when I did return to the force and was able to gain a much clearer picture of the type of cases which regularly faced female officers. It was an area which concerned me, and in future years a 'specialist' course was arranged for women to receive appropriate training and role play to help in taking statements, especially from female victims of sexual offences or domestic abuse.

All the recruits, both male and female officers, had already received their uniforms, but at the end of the training programme the men were also issued with truncheons and handcuffs to help them in their daily battle against crime. Us women officers received neither. I rather hoped that my fellow female officers and I would never need any weapon for protection or restraints for calming down offenders – after all, we still had our whistles with which to apprehend any violent criminals!

Whilst there was a competitive camaraderie among the recruits during our 13 weeks, our paths rarely crossed in future years as many came from the provincial forces in the north-west whilst my own 'backyard' was very much in the north-east of England, in the North Riding and northwards up towards Northumberland. It was to this neck of the woods that I made my return journey. Next stop for me, as a newly trained officer: Richmond.

CHAPTER 4

NORTH RIDING
THE FIRST RUNG OF
THE LADDER

My feelings as I arrived at Richmond, suitcase in hand containing my carefully pressed new uniform, were of absolute pride. I felt elated, I had achieved the first of my ambitions and was now a fully fledged member of the North Riding police force.

Richmond was a busy market town situated well away from any major industrial conurbations with life revolving very much around the agricultural community and farming in general. Market day was the highlight of the week and in truth my time spent working there (only two months) was generally uneventful, providing a gentle introduction to the world of policing and serving the community. I didn't anticipate Richmond to be the epicentre of crime, harbouring 'bad 'uns' at every corner... and so it proved. Near to Richmond was the Catterick army camp, so in the very unlikely event of any outbreak of violent pensioner squabbles over the price of potatoes, we had several hundred soldiers close at hand who could be called upon to intervene!

In many respects my first day proved most memorable. I stepped out of my lodgings, half a mile away from the police station, wearing my new uniform, which became my daily clothes of necessity and choice. Perhaps not the preferred selection of every 20-year-old single woman at the time, but to me my uniform represented the smart efficiency of someone who could command respect, ooze confidence and be trusted by people with whom she came into contact. The epitome of smartness and robustness: a dark navy blue semi-fitted jacket with chrome buttons, a smart straight skirt, crisp white shirt with loose collar and collar studs, black tie, black rayon stockings (not the harder-wearing nylons!) and sturdy black leather lace-up shoes. All topped off with a smart cap.

Did the uniform look smart and efficient? Yes, definitely. Was it comfortable? Yes, generally. Was the uniform fashionable? Hmm, yes, depending on your point of view. Was the uniform practical? Well, despite what you may have thought, actually no, not really; the skirt was straight, making it very difficult to run, as your legs simply couldn't move far enough forwards or backwards. And as for climbing ladders, well, I'll deal with that one later!

The clothing was never meant to be a fashion statement; it was meant to show a smart woman in uniform, looking and feeling efficient even though little thought had been given to its practicalities. That would only come when Miss de Vitré got more closely involved and saw at first hand the practical difficulties of the uniform. She was able to introduce the first of several changes which took effect over the coming years and decades. Several years into my career during the 1960s, I was also able to introduce my own set of uniform modifications. When I was established in Northumberland, trousers and handbags became an integral part of the women's police wardrobe and not before time.

I recall having discussions with my Inspector during my early years, who had chastised me because my jacket pockets were bulging – I remember he referred rather rudely to 'those saddlebags!' I had to explain that my pockets were bulging only because there was nowhere else on my uniform in which to keep my whistle, keys, pocketbook, tape measure, pen, chalk and so on… Yes, a handbag to contain working essentials would have been very helpful. A policeman had trousers with pockets as well as a jacket with pockets; Perhaps this was another case of a lack of thought rather than a deliberate act of inequality.

I kept my own mantra: 'Look smart, feel smart, look efficient' despite having some frustrations with the early impractical nature of the uniform. This was a guide which helped me throughout my career, simply because people would have confidence and respect me more than if I dressed shabbily or looked slovenly. Even to this day, my shoes are always polished. Quite simply, it leaves a good impression.

Anyway, back to that first operational day as a police constable. I was ready to change the world: well, my world at least! That morning I left the station and made my way on a two-minute walk to the court building. Whilst on route I saw my very first unlawful situation as a member of the law enforcement and took immediate action. A car was parked at the side of the road; I glanced briefly towards it and with mixed emotions of shock and trepidation, I noticed it had failed to display a road tax disc! My response was immediate and forceful – I wrote down all the car details in my pocket book – make, model, colour and registration number – and my very first case was up and running. OK, perhaps I'd acted as though this was an eagerly awaited moment for making an impression but it was hardly the crime-busting, headline-grabbing news that would enthral the law-abiding citizens of Richmond. However small in the scheme of things, this act did nevertheless, herald the start of my attempts in making the world a better and safer place for everyday folk to enjoy!

From the very start, it was made quite clear to me that I was first and foremost a police officer. No concessions were to be given because I was a woman. Every day a full 15 minutes before our shift began, we had to go on parade for inspection and be given a brief for our respective beats. I worked a beat just like my male colleagues and had to make points at telephone kiosks along the route every half hour. These telephone kiosks or special police boxes which were introduced in some urban areas, were in effect a 'miniature police station' for use by police officers to read and fill in reports, take meal breaks or even temporarily hold detainees until the arrival of transport. The blue kiosks had a light on top of the box which would flash to alert any patrolling officer that they were to contact the station. These police boxes were invariably located near to the red telephone kiosks of the period and in the absence of personal radios and several decades before the advent of mobile phones, this was the only way that communication between officers on patrol and the station could happen.

One day whilst I was making a point at a telephone box, I noticed that the Chief Constable's car drew up and stopped outside the box. I immediately stood to attention and was on edge wondering why on earth the Chief Constable would want to stop and see me. 'What had I done wrong?' was my immediate thought. I looked again and it was Lieutenant Colonel Chaytor who had made the original application to the Home Office for me to be considered for joining the police force. He simply wanted to congratulate me on my positive report from the Training Centre at Bruche. What a lovely gesture of him and a true mark of the man for whom I had real respect. Moments after he had driven away, the station's sergeant appeared out of nowhere, demanding to know what the Chief Constable wanted with me!

I was the only woman in the division which covered the Catterick Camp and was always on call in case a woman officer was required to attend the camp. Whilst I did not have a night shift in these early weeks of my tenure, I had to remain on call and be available just in case a woman officer was needed to deal with any issues requiring female specific presence.

Indeed, throughout my working life, this became a common thread, and, in many respects, it could be said that I was virtually married into the police force. Simply, it had to take priority over everything because I had to be on hand to deal with any issues in which I was required to get involved, whatever the time of day... or night. Yes, on reflection, perhaps this may have curtailed what else I could do, especially in my younger years, when I sometimes missed going out with friends to the pub, to the cinema or to dances. I guess it was a bit disruptive if I had been on a date and I had to leave halfway through or sometimes before the date had even begun! But I had made my decision and I was happy with it and I was still able to have a good time when I wanted, as long as I was always ready for the unexpected phone call or make myself available to move to a new part of the country to collect a prisoner.

My stay at Richmond, although short and largely uneventful, did, however, provide my introduction to those areas of the police service which catered for neglected children and missing girls. I also learnt how to take responsibility for looking after women prisoners and searching them before leading them to their cells. This was a new experience, but I have always felt that a female officer's involvement does generally help to calm situations and often removes any threat of violence or aggression from occurring.

My two months in Richmond were quickly over as I received a new posting a few miles away towards the north-east coast and on to Scarborough. It was the start of the year, in readiness to prepare for the busy spring, summer season and it had been decreed that the one current female officer required assistance. Here I was stepping into that role. I went into lodgings with Mr and Mrs Edwards, who treated me very kindly and made me feel completely at home. I remember that they owned a shop during the period of rationing, so we rarely went without sugar or butter, which were in short supply. They didn't have children of their own, but always looked after me very well. I still have and own the Ronson cigarette lighter which they had given me on my 21st birthday. A kind, generous and lovely couple who made me feel completely relaxed and welcome. It was an ideal new home from which I could face a new dynamic and the hustle and bustle of a popular seaside resort destination.

Scarborough gave me a broader understanding of how women had been accepted into the force and opened my eyes to new areas of police involvement to which I had previously never been privy. Up until recently, Scarborough had been a relatively small borough force, but amalgamations of these smaller forces were starting to take place more rapidly, in order to provide greater stability and consistency across regions. Hence it had been no real surprise when the Scarborough force was incorporated within the North Riding, leaving several officers still serving there who clearly resented the change. It was a sign of the times.

There were several officers who felt aggrieved that their small force had suddenly been transformed into a much bigger unit, which commanded greater discipline and increased levels of reporting authority, so perhaps some felt their 'toes had been stood on' and they had lost some independence or levels of responsibility. It was certainly the start of a bigger period of change. Structures within the provincial police forces were certainly being modified, and there was an increased number of women officers being recruited into forces. As a result it was a period of transition, designed to make the whole police organisation nationwide more cohesive and effective.

Scarborough was a very busy summer resort with a huge influx of holidaymakers from around the country between May and September. This required a proportionate arrival of new, part-time workers to help service the tourist population surge over these summer months, mainly in the hotel and catering services. This meant it was a busy time for us as police officers as well, dealing with lots of petty crimes. Many of these involved small pilferages from hotels and shops where the holidaymakers and new workers were residing, as well as several fraud cases. Thankfully there was very little in the way of 'meaty' cases to pursue, but there were a couple of new experiences during my time in Scarborough which I'd like to share.

I had never previously visited a coroner's office, but it struck me that a postmortem was a very necessary procedure when investigating any untimely, sudden or suspicious deaths. This meant it would be in the interests of my own self-development and investigative education to understand exactly what was involved at the coroner's office. There was an official Coroner's Officer (a member of the police force) based in Scarborough, so I asked him if I could attend a postmortem at a time when I was not on duty. This was quickly agreed, but leading up to the appointment, I was filled with nervous tension and trepidation at not being able to cope with the unknown and possibly macabre scenes I was to behold. I simply had no idea what to expect, but as with many new and potentially unpleasant experiences I realised I had to resist the temptation not to attend and simply 'get on with it'. Another mantra of mine, which I followed throughout my career.

As things turned out, the postmortem was such an interesting experience and a huge eye-opener. In many respects, the methodical and logical procedures carried out by the coroner looking for unusual signs on a body to help identify the cause of death, is very much in parallel with police officers looking for clues when trying to solve a crime. This occasion helped me in future years to consider postmortems not as an invasive study of someone's dead body, but rather as nothing more than a very necessary investigation, thereby providing much needed answers to as yet unsolved riddles.

The second of my Scarborough 'firsts' occurred shortly after my arrival. There had been several complaints received at the police station about a nuisance individual who felt it necessary to expose himself to unsuspecting women who were walking through the delightful Valley Gardens in the middle of Scarborough. We needed to arrest this public menace, so I was instructed to go to the Valley Gardens in civilian clothes whilst being supposedly shadowed by a male officer. My policewoman colleague had done this the previous four evenings without the menace making an appearance, so it was now my turn.

As it transpired, I had not ventured very far into the gardens when a man wearing a long raincoat appeared and started walking towards me. He suddenly stopped and as I anticipated opened his coat and exposed himself. As a 21-year-old woman, it was a frightening experience to be confronted with this 'flasher', not knowing what he may try to do next. It became more frightening when I looked around but could not see any sign of the male officer who was supposedly shadowing me. Nevertheless, I had to persevere, so I plucked up enough courage to explain that I was a police officer and was arresting him for indecent exposure with intent to insult a female. I had no personal radio, no truncheon to protect myself and I was in civilian clothes without any immediate backup, but thankfully he gave me the respect that an officer warranted. After a little persuasion, he resisted no more and I was able to arrest him, albeit without handcuffs as women officers had not yet been granted them; no mobile phone either.

It occurred to me at the time that I had been taught through my police training that a police officer must always be able to show the evidence of a crime to his or her sergeant. Hence I look back with some amusement that after arresting him, I told him that he was not to pull up his trousers, so that the Sergeant at the station could see that he was in a state of undress as his indecency crime determined. I then realised that I couldn't very well walk him to the station with trousers around his ankles! I made a compromise and let him pull up his trousers without fastening the front; at the same time, I hailed down a passing taxi and rather shakily was able to take him down to the station where my Sergeant was able to see quite clearly the evidence of the offence in question! The man appeared in court and was subsequently convicted of two charges of indecent exposure whilst the magistrates commended me for my perseverance, bravery and attention to duty in making this arrest. Looking back, it was January when the incident took place – I'm only surprised that nuisance never got a touch of frostbite as a result. That would certainly have taught him a lesson!

As I mentioned earlier, Scarborough was extremely busy during the summer and there were many petty crimes carried out by both men and women. Female offenders were sent to Durham Prison, which caused the police service some difficulties since there was no transport in the division. This meant that women prisoners had to be taken there by train. On one such occasion I was given the rather daunting task of escorting not one, but two women from Scarborough to Durham by public train whilst also having to change trains in York, with prisoners in tow. As a still relatively raw 21-year-old rookie, it did prove a little uncomfortable knowing that two women would probably be able to overpower me in a struggle if one ever arose. Nevertheless, by talking straight and keeping vigilant, I made it safely to Durham with my cargo of two prisoners fully intact. I really couldn't see a single female police officer exposed to that sort of risk in today's world, without any weapons – not even a truncheon to protect herself – but back then we just got on with it!

Summertime was enjoyable in Scarborough but there was a massive transformation in the winter months when the tourists had returned home, the vocational workers left to spend their wages and we police officers were left tidying up the administration from the summer of criminal activity and very little else. So, when I had my assessment it was with some delight that I agreed to move away from Scarborough but stay within the North Riding force with a move to my next post at Northallerton.

When I arrived I found I was the only woman in the Division so I was instructed to attend any matters requiring a female officer. This always meant I needed to be on call, so any private life was suddenly less private.

I was also required to carry out the same role as the men in the station. This didn't faze me because I was ambitious and craved new experiences so as a 22-year-old woman, I worked the beat as any of my male colleagues did. At the station two of us worked each night, splitting time equally between being in the office and out on the beat. The two working shifts were between 10pm and 2am and then from 2am to 6am and on occasions we reversed the shifts the following night. I have to be honest and admit that it was all a little frightening, as I often felt very isolated with no personal radio, no backup support, no car and no truncheon (I only carried my large rubber torch!). In the pitch darkness of night, it was eerie having to check shop doors, especially if they were unlocked, or worse still, ajar. It happened one night at a cinema, which when empty is a big place and at night seemed very shadowy and dangerous and especially so when the front doors were unlocked! I felt a little fearful at times, but it was so important to keep your nerve and not to be spooked into submission and panic. A quick look around with my torch – very quick mind you – and then closing the doors very firmly was normally all that it took and a note to talk to the owners the following morning.

At the time, I was living in lodgings in Northallerton and my landlord took it upon himself to tell his friends that I was patrolling at night around the town and on my own, without any real protection from either the elements or from any potential undesirables. They decided they would complain to the Chief Constable out of a sense of duty that it was not right for a young woman to be out on her own at night patrolling the streets in efforts to safeguard others. They wanted to highlight public perception and interest and as a result of their complaint, my duties did become more varied with less emphasis on night patrol. Whilst I had made the single nightly patrols without question or argument, I must say that I have never come across any other female officer patrolling the streets at night unless accompanied by another officer, so I was rather indebted to the kindness of my landlord and his friends for highlighting the issues and raising their own concerns.

It soon became apparent that I was very much accepted by my male colleagues in Northallerton, which the following incident illustrates quite clearly, I think. A male colleague was showing me around a new beat at midnight. We were at a crossroads with a public house situated over the road from where we were standing. The PC turned to me and said that if you sit on this wall and look directly over towards the pub, you will often find that the landlord's daughter will get undressed, at around this time, leaving the curtains wide open! You can imagine my response: 'If you think I'm going to sit here in the cold waiting to see what I can see every night in front of the mirror, then you're mistaken!' The officer had relaxed with me as his colleague to the extent that he treated me as if I was any other male officer in the force!

I have always enjoyed looking back retrospectively at my early years, especially when I became Assistant at the

Inspectorate and started visiting the provincial forces around the country and interviewing many women serving as police officers. On one such occasion I returned to Northallerton and could relate to them by asking if they still left a glass of milk out at Cow & Gate or could you call at the bakery for tea and cake before the shift ended at 6am. They could see you had been there and done it and worked your way up through the force, just like they were doing.

I have always felt it was extremely important to be able to show by example that you started where others are now, and only by working to the best of your ability have you been able to move onwards and upwards. It gives people hope and aspirations. I always felt the same about Miss de Vitré and I always looked up to her and admired how she used her wisdom to such good effect and in such a positive manner when talking to eager, willing officers, like I was at the time.

It was during my time in Northallerton that I encountered a very distressing case of incest as I was quickly introduced to a very different side of life. The fact that a father can victimise and disrespect his own flesh and blood made a big impression on me, as I came to realise how some people lived in a very dark and disturbing side of society. This was such a far cry from my own 'normal' upbringing and I often wondered how I and others had been sheltered from such harrowing and heart-breaking horrors within a family group.

During the same period and within a short space of time, I had arrested two people, one for shoplifting and one who had committed indecent assault. On both occasions and before either had appeared in court, tragically they both committed suicide. This had a massive effect on me as I started questioning myself and what I was doing. Here I was, only three or four years into my career, and I felt as though I already had two peoples' lives on my conscience. I questioned my job – was I doing the right thing and was this profession really for me? My working environment – why should I expose myself to so many awful situations? My faith – how could such awful things be allowed to happen and did issues arising at work conflict with my faith?

In fact, I had reached a 'low', and entered a short but 'dark period' for me in my young life. I'd always had a strong faith and was a regular churchgoer, so I had always felt 'guided' by the principles in which I lived and the faith I followed. Recent events at that time were now questioning the core values of those principles and my faith.

'Battling on' is a well-versed phrase and one which rings true for me during this period. Whilst feeling quite low I was given the opportunity of a fresh challenge, still within the North Riding, but this time in South Bank, a rigidly and tradi-tional industrial and working-class area near Middlesbrough. This gave me the opportunity to reflect. With the help of my local GP, I accepted the job and with it the challenges it would bring me as a person, facing unknown situations and dealing with many very different and often very complex people.

CHAPTER 5

SOUTH BANK
A MASSIVE INFLUENCE

South Bank was a hard place: a tough suburb of Middlesbrough situated three miles from the town centre on the banks of the River Tees and a short distance from the Eston Hills. The iron and steel industries had grown up around this area, taking raw iron ore from the mineral-rich hills surrounding the various industrial works. When I arrived there as a foot patrol police officer, it was very clear to me that this was a tough, no nonsense, working-class environment where the men grafted through their physically hard shifts in the steel manufacturing industry or on the shipbuilding docks and often in dank, dirty conditions. At the sound of the siren which signalled the end of the working shift, the workers moved en masse from their work to the public houses, where the pints of beer were already lined up on the counter.

This in many respects typified the way of life – hard physical encounters with tough resilient people who worked hard, played hard but sometimes let their aggressions go too far. It was certainly a hard living, with money (or lack of it) often an issue and sometimes dominant males in the household taking advantage of situations and letting their bullying instincts take over.

There were two women officers at South Bank and we both lived in the same lodgings, working opposite shifts, but not nights. If a woman officer was needed when neither of us were on duty, then we were both on call, so one of us was always available. We always had to provide details of our whereabouts when we were off duty, so it was not unusual to see a display on the cinema screen asking for the policewoman to report to the police station at the earliest opportunity! It was not unusual to be called out at any time of night as well.

It was very clear to me. The job came first, and it was important that I always had that sense of priority of the job over family and personal matters. I'm sure I lost out on certain things at the expense of my police career and despite my success in reaching the top of my profession, it is also true that everything comes at a cost. I'm sure this was in my thinking when I ultimately retired from work at the 'youngish' age of 49 so that I could spend the rest of my adult life doing what I wanted to do, without the constraints of being available to the service 24 hours a day.

Back to South Bank. Each officer worked a beat on their own, making points every half hour at listed telephone kiosks. I've always believed in police officers working a beat because it provides the opportunity for them to talk to people, to get to know them and to build relationships. This means building bridges and gaining the confidence of the people.

In years which followed, when there was a shortage of officers which ultimately led to foot patrol being replaced by panda car patrol, I really felt there was a loss of contact and service. A loss of gossiping on the grass verge finding out what was happening in the locality; knowing who was vulnerable and lonely, who was looking as though they were under great stress and who may have been carrying injuries and were possible victims of domestic abuse. In South Bank our foot patrols provided an excellent opportunity to enjoy mixing with people from all districts and it proved ideal for relationship building and gaining a mutual understanding and respect which had been hitherto lacking.

Getting closer to the community was the key as far as I was concerned, because it felt as though I was helping to make a difference on a personal level as well as through my profession. My role as a police officer was not all about taking the bad people out from society and putting them behind bars. It was as much about helping those who were surviving under the immense pressures and strains in their everyday, normal working lives. It was becoming more commonplace for us to be called to domestic disputes and allegations of abuse. On one such occasion, we turned up to a house where a woman was walking around naked in the road because her husband had burned all her clothes. The reason why? She had spent all the housekeeping money, not frittered it away on extravagant items, merely spent it before the week was over and before the next pay packet was available.

She clearly needed some help managing the household budget and this form of domestic bullying was certainly not going to aid matters, so I took it upon myself to assist her. I spent time with her during this period and visited her house over a few Friday evenings to help her understand the budgeting principles for her household, highlighting what were the priority daily essentials and what were not classed as everyday necessities. It took a little time to teach her how to manage her money more carefully, but it worked, and I found the whole process very satisfying. I felt I'd made a difference for this lady who had been a victim of some very unnecessary abuse.

By walking the beat, we would work more closely with people in the community and over time got to know them well. One of my favourite beats in South Bank took me past some allotments where I often took time to chat with several of the older men who were working there. They were my eyes and ears of the neighbourhood and would pass on any concerns they had about people who may have been in difficulties and who we in turn would try and help. It was only through conversation and building up trust that barriers were broken down and mutual assistance could be given and received. The men at the allotment often showed their appreciation and friendliness by passing me an egg or two which one of their chickens had laid. What did I do with the eggs whilst I walked the rest of my beat? Well, I placed them safely under my hat, safe in the knowledge that the cap had quite a hard exterior and would be a safe nesting place until I got them home and served them up for my tea!

Me as a fresh-faced 20-year-old trainee at the
Police Training centre in Bruche where it all began.

Enjoying a weekly discussion with colleagues whilst attending a course at the Police College for sergeants qualified to be promoted to the level of inspector. I was one of only three women who attended out of a group of 150 officers.

HMI inspection at the Middlesbrough police station in the early 1960s.

The District
Inspectors' course
took place at
Solberge Hall, North
Riding Training
Centre 1962.

Presenting awards
at the National
Police Sports Day
in Gateshead in the
early 1970s.

The Northumberland Constabulary First Aid team with a pile of silverware after winning several regional and national competitions.

During my time at the Home Office I enjoyed travelling around the country to visit the provincial forces and carry out inspections. Here I am meeting members of the West Yorkshire force during my rounds in 1979.

Miss Barbara Denis de Vitré: the first female police officer to hold the position of Assistant to Chief HMI.

My move to the Home Office in 1978 saw me initially working as Staff Officer to the Assistant Inspector of Constabulary. Within a year I was promoted to the position of Assistant to Chief HMI, following in the footsteps of the woman who had been a huge inspiration to me: Miss Denis de Vitré. She was the first and I was the last person to hold this position in the police force.

I was very proud to have met the Queen Mother at the
Metropolitan Policewomen's 60th anniversary dinner in 1979.
I was the only non-Metropolitan officer present as I represented
the provincial police forces. Here I am with officers from
the Met along with the Queen Mother.

Standing outside Alnwick Castle with my mother, my
sister May, my niece Jen, and my great nephew Mark,
shortly after receiving my Queen's Police Medal in 1979.

One of the joys of retirement has been to relax on holiday both at home and abroad. Here I am with my very good friend Joan Harnby, enjoying the sunshine of the Sahara, moments before riding off on one of the camels you see in the background!

Mind you, it was certainly not all plain sailing. There were occasions when I had to change tack and move away from being polite, reasonable and courteous, to shocking people into taking notice. One such time I had been responding to a domestic incident involving a couple who were screaming abuse at each other using extremely dreadful language. Despite several attempts, my firm but polite requests for them to calm down and lower their tone were completely ignored. I was left with little option as they were becoming a public nuisance, so against my normal nature, I changed tone and suddenly shouted at them very forcefully and a little rudely so that they stopped in their tracks. I had reacted in a way they had not expected but their verbal assault on each other stopped abruptly. It was another good lesson for me to learn.

My time spent at South Bank was a massive learning curve and I felt very fulfilled in my work, especially after my feelings of depression during my latter time at Northallerton. It provided an education and grounding which I would simply never have got anywhere else. I learnt very important lessons about relationships, empathy and developing my own intuition to differentiate between deliberate criminal acts and the harsh reality of surviving in often very difficult circumstances.

As a police force, we got quite close to some families, especially in cases where the mother and her children were the innocent victims of domestic abuse by a rogue husband and father. In one family in particular, the father was a habitual petty thief who regularly broke into the gas meters to steal money, which ultimately led to convictions and regular spells in prison. This left his wife, Minnie, with their children to carry on as best they could, surviving on very little indeed. In some respects, we at the police station 'adopted' the family when he was 'inside' and often made regular visits to Minnie with essentials and goodies to help make her and her children's existence more bearable.

Some five years later, when I returned to Middlesbrough as an Inspector, there was some publicity about my return in the *Evening Gazette*, the local paper. It touched my heartstrings when the first person to visit and welcome me at my new office at Police HQ was Minnie, along with several of her children! She was not bitter about the fact that the police had often apprehended her husband, but instead had remembered my kindness in supporting her and wanted to show her appreciation by welcoming me at the police station itself!

I really felt that as women officers, it was important that we showed we were very much aware of the difficulties facing women at this particular time in the mid-1950s, and that we should try and help as best we could. One of our regular duties was to attend the domestic court, which was held every month and saw domestic issues dealt with by magistrates.

In many cases of domestic abuse physical violence had been dished out by the perpetrator, invariably the husband against the wife, and she had come to the station in a battered state with a multitude of cuts and bruises. Invariably and sadly, the case was ultimately dropped by the victim before it could reach court. Why? Simply because the victim had nowhere else to turn, except to go back home and live with the reality of ongoing abuse. Society back in the fifties and early sixties did not have the infrastructure of protection groups to deal properly with such offences.

Domestic abuse, affiliation orders and separation orders were the common topics. I remember one solicitor saying to me, 'No wonder you don't get married, listening to all this!' How true.

Society was different back then in the mid-20th century and barely a decade after the end of the most terrible war the world had ever seen. There was very little help for families, and in court, if orders were made for payment to be made, invariably it was not forthcoming. There were families who would take the husband's suit to the pawn shop on Monday morning to receive cash and then when the wages came out on Friday, they would retrieve the suit so the husband could wear it to go out on the Saturday night. This was the way many people in working-class areas lived, when the labour was very physical, demanding, and sometimes hard to come by and money for the household was often tight.

Dealing with unacceptable behaviour by juveniles was a challenging issue but was one we had to face head-on during my time in South Bank. Again, holding out a hand of friendship and guidance during volatile times for this sector of the community allowed us to better understand their issues and hopefully help them reform their behaviour along the way. We arranged for groups of juveniles with behavioural issues to come along to the police station and play table tennis amongst themselves and a few of the officers. Some of them even met me on a Sunday morning at 8am and then accompanied me to church before my duties started an hour later.

I am proud of my time helping build relationships in the community, not only with vulnerable members of the public, but also with support groups like the NSPCC, the Children's Department and with probation officers. This is where I felt the police service and particularly female police officers could really make a difference, so it became a significant focus for me as my career in the police force developed over the next 25 or so years. But it was here, in South Bank, that this cooperative, multi-faceted approach started to take effect to protect and also to help and serve the community. I built relationships with the churches in the locality and it was not uncommon for the local Catholic priest to ask if we had any of his flock at the station! The network created between us and the parish churches enabled us to start working together and supporting each other in efforts to help the local community function safely and more effectively.

In highly industrialised towns and especially ports like South Bank, there was a very high proportion of men working and often away from the comforts of their family and home. So it was likely that the local population would try to help serve these newcomers to the town. Local infrastructure like shops and pubs were clearly part of the service, but so too was the oldest profession of them all: prostitution.

As a police service, we had to deal with prostitution and the perilous conditions in which these women lived and worked. The seedy nature of their business, because the 'work' was carried out in dark and dingy surroundings, meant that it was a dangerous profession for women to get involved in. By talking directly to the prostitutes, we found out that many were in the profession out of desperation to put food on the table for themselves and often for their children.

There has been so much debate over the years about the rights and wrongs of prostitution, but one thing is for sure: there is a huge demand in certain areas. This brings with it the need for some kind of legalised quality-controlled enterprise which allows women to work in safe and hygienic conditions with regular health checks for the sake of themselves and their partners. I saw at first hand the dangers open to prostitutes and knew that if prostitution as a crime was clamped down on even more harshly, then punters and prostitutes would be driven even further underground and that would only further exacerbate the social problem. Added to that, if prostitution is not available, there is the likelihood of a potential increase in sexual offences and attacks on innocent women. It's a very difficult subject and one that really demands extensive discussion before considering legalised prostitution in our modern civilised society. There are obvious moral rights and wrongs which should be debated in the context of social needs within a law-abiding culture.

Faced with the certainty that prostitutes were a fact of life, it was important that again we talked – female police officer to prostitute, woman to woman – to understand the issues whilst keeping safety as the priority. It was our challenge and priority to reduce incidents of innocents, like children, getting involved and to prevent any dangers and threats of violence from occurring.

Prostitution was rife in South Bank, especially down at the jetty where there were frequent moorings of container ships from around Europe and Scandinavia in particular. This was a haven for prostitutes because there was an abundant supply of potential customers lined up in a relatively safe and comfortable environment. As a result, when the vessel came to sail and the Captain asked the prostitutes to leave, it was not uncommon for the women to refuse and sometimes even try and hide away on board. Prior to my arrival this had always resulted in a call from the captain which led to a posse of male police officers, often rather heavy-handed, escorting the prostitutes from the ship. Prostitutes felt they had every right to be there on the ship as they had been granted access onto private property in the first place. This had done little to help foster a line of communication between the police and the prostitutes, which could ultimately be of mutual benefit.

I was aware of this difficult and problematic relationship as well as the need to build bridges and constructive dialogue, not worsen the conflict. I felt that involvement from myself and the other female officer may help reduce friction and even help build towards a greater understanding. I carried out some research and established that the jetty differed from the docks at Middlesbrough, three miles upriver, because the Merchant Shipping Act did apply to the boats at the jetty and consequently the law of trespass was in place. This effectively meant that the girls could be prosecuted in court if they did not leave the vessel when requested by the captain. Clearly this could have curtailed their business if there was a custodial sentence or damaged their purse in the case of a fine. It certainly helped make sure in the future that the prostitutes rarely outstayed their welcome on the ships at the jetty and invariably left at the captain's request.

I discussed this issue with my Inspector, and we agreed that the female officers would go on board the ship at the next altercation. We would make the arrests, even though we were accompanied by the male officers. The first time that I and my female colleague boarded the ship, we were looked upon by the ship's crew in a rather questioning manner – were we real police officers or merely prostitute replacements in uniform? Searching for offenders was not particularly easy on a vessel with many interlinking rooms, doors and corridors, but on this first occasion we found 'Jenny', one of the intended stow-aways with her sailor. Both were naked and refusing to get off the boat. Despite her uncooperative approach and the rather vulgar way she told our Inspector to clear off, we did succeed in allowing the ship to sail away without any female South Bank inhabitants on board!

After this, we were always involved and after an initially rather testing period of tension between us and the prostitutes, we spent time getting to know them and began looking out for their welfare, whilst keeping a 'blind' eye on proceedings when it was necessary. They proved to be a wealth of informa-tion and were often very good, reliable informants especially on the whereabouts of youngsters who may have got caught up inadvertently in 'the game'. Starting this type of communi-cation in South Bank served me very well when I returned to

Middlesbrough several years later during a period when missing children had become a bigger priority. I was able to call on the knowledge of the prostitutes to help us turn young girls away from a life of possible prostitution. More of that later.

Fuelled by everything I was learning on the job, I still harboured aspirations for my own career development. At the earliest opportunity (which was becoming a trademark of mine) I started studying for my promotion exams to attain the level of sergeant. I could take these once I had achieved four years' service in the police force.

I duly sat and passed the Sergeant's Entrance Exam in 1954 and started looking at potential placement opportunities immediately afterwards. A post was advertised in Northumberland county, so I duly requested permission from my Chief Constable to apply. He declined my request! Unfortunately for me, regulations required that I have five years' service under my belt unless there were special circumstances. With my police officer experiences having been solely in the North Riding, my Chief Constable explained that had there been a vacancy within this force he would not hesitate as my accomplishments were well known in this force and I knew all the relevant policies and procedures for the district. An opening for a sergeant position in the North Riding was not available. Different district forces still operated autonomously with little consistency or uniformity across any of the provincial forces. This may have put me in a vulnerable position from the start, especially given the regulations specifically indicated five years before a promotion could take effect. I accepted that I would need to wait a little longer.

Shortly afterwards, I was selected to attend a CID (Criminal Investigation Department) training course in Wakefield which added to my depth of police knowledge and proved invaluable experience as I paved my way to progress through the police ranks. I didn't have to wait too long before my opportunity arose, as the Northumberland position was advertised again. I applied and was accepted, subject to passing the medical. That itself proved a little awkward and embarrassing initially, as I was covered in flea bites. The police surgeon fully understood as he had worked in South Bank as a doctor and knew full well that I had been working among the fleas. The landlady at my digs used to have clothes in the shed ready for me when I came off duty, thereby allowing me to leave my uniform in the shed to be de-bugged. Such were the hazards in police work!

As a result of passing the interview (and the medical), and following five years of patrolling the streets of North Yorkshire in Richmond, Scarborough, Northallerton and South Bank, I had gained my first promotion, to the rank of Sergeant in the county of Northumberland. The 1st of December 1955 heralded a new start for me – and an important one too – it was my first occasion of being given the task and responsibility of managing people.

CHAPTER 6

GOSFORTH
MY FIRST
SUPERVISORY POST

Sergeant Sigsworth had a nice-sounding, alliterative ring to it which rolled off the tongue very easily. It felt good. I had attained my first promotion and was now charting new territory, not just in my new job spec but also in a new provincial police force.

My new office 'home' in the Northumberland Constabulary was at the Gosforth Division, where I had the responsibility for all the women officers in the division, even though they worked under the command of the male supervisory officers. It was a big step for me as well as something of a change for the division, as I had stepped in to become the first female Sergeant in the team.

Working together proved to be the key during my near four and a half years in this suburb of Newcastle and in the county of Northumberland, and the diverse experiences I had there heavily reinforced what I'd learnt about life in the force.

As women officers we had responsibility for dealing with all the sudden deaths in the mental hospital, each of which required a postmortem examination. As we were coroner's officers, we had to attend each session. Whilst as previously mentioned it was a fascinating experience to attend a postmortem, at the same time it was not necessarily something that you would choose to attend regularly. One pathologist insisted we also had to take notes of all his findings during his observations which drew us even closer to his dissection of the body. Not an overly pleasant task for the officers, male or female, to have to carry out.

As part of the county force, the Gosforth Division officers also had to attend courtroom regularly. The courts of assize were periodic courts normally held on a quarterly basis to hear the more serious criminal and civil cases, whilst the more minor offences, both civil and criminal, were dealt with by local Justices of the Peace in petty sessions, also known as the magistrates court. The courtroom for Gosforth was in the city of Newcastle, at the Moothall, and it was our duty to police this area. A woman was always on duty in both assize courts when they were sitting, which had also been the case when the assize courts sat at York when I had been in the North Riding.

I recall one occasion when I was sitting in the civil court at York and my female colleague was sitting opposite in the criminal court. When my case was adjourned, I noticed that my colleague was sitting outside the crown court, which struck me as rather unusual. On asking her why, she told me that the judge had requested all ladies to leave the courtroom as they were about to try a rather nasty bestiality case. Naturally in her professional capacity, the female officer stayed in court until the judge turned to her and said, 'Are policewomen no longer ladies?', at which point she left the court. The judge was clearly being courteous and showing old-fashioned respect for all women, including female officers.

I first worked with young offenders in South Bank, and it quickly became a cornerstone of my time spent in Gosforth. Within the district there was a senior girls' approved school, St Hilda's in Salters Road, which had various guises over many years and was originally run as a home for sisterhood and formed under the auspices of the Church Penitentiary Association. In the 1950s the premises were available for juvenile girls between the ages of 15 and 17 who may have been in need of care, protection or control. Alternatively, pupils might have been found guilty of an offence which, in the case of an adult, could be punished by a prison sentence. In reality, quite often the girls had run away from the care of a Local Authority or played truant and now needed some help reforming to get ready to join society as young women. The inmates were occupied in domestic training skills and gardening, with much effort designed to prevent them from becoming a risk by falling into sexual promiscuity or prostitution.

Many of the girls were unruly, so it wasn't a great surprise that some of them managed to abscond on a regular basis. The women officers from the police station started interviewing the girls after their eventual return to find out the reasons for disappearing and to find out what they had got up to during their period of 'freedom'. The Headmistress, Miss Bird, was tough, firm but fair and very much in charge. The girls respected her authority and when confronted, invariably answered truthfully. They were often asked what they had been up to during the time they had been away with direct questions along the lines of, 'Did you steal it?'....'Did you sell your body?" Such was her air of authority and control, the girls invariably answered immediately with a resounding, 'Yes, Miss Bird'.

Over time, I became more involved, attending the school frequently and taking communion in the school's chapel on a Thursday morning before going on duty, whilst also getting to know some of the girls held there. Many of the girls were from Teesside and I may well have come across them in my previous post, in South Bank. During my time at Gosforth I became a member of the management committee itself and consequently became better acquainted with the staff and the reforming girls. I was able to provide some directional and meaningful input, all geared towards steering a positive reformation for all the girls held within.

I returned to Northumberland as Chief Inspector a few years later. Miss Bird had passed away and there was a new Headmistress at the school. One night there was a riot at St Hilda's School and on visiting the old Victorian building, there were girls hanging out of the windows in various state of undress. Standing at the door was the curate looking exasperated and forlorn, whilst the female officers escorted the girls out of the windows and down the ladders, whilst holding onto their nighties. The house had been wrecked so we had no alternative but to put the girls into custody across the region. The Superintendent at that time, a broad Scot, was advised of the situation and he turned to me and said, 'Well, if they'd let the lads in, there would have been no problem. If the cows get restless in the fields, you turn in the bulls!'

The local vicar used to take the Eucharist (communion) service every Thursday at 8am. Many years later and after my retirement, when I was a churchwarden in Maidenhead, I was asked to pick up an exchange priest from New Zealand. I met him and his wife at Heathrow and during our conversation, I discovered he had served his curacy at Gosforth so knew the reform school very well. What a small world!

There was an instance I can remember when we tried to seek help for a young tearaway who was often out of control, so her parents simply couldn't restrain her. We were asked to offer advice and wanted to take her to court to find the best outcome for her. However, before that could happen, there was a direct intervention from the Jewish Board of Guardians, who immediately had the girl removed and put under their control, whilst they chastised me for getting involved in the first place. I had very little involvement with crimes by Jewish people during my career, and this really served to show that they liked to look after their own and in their own way, wherever possible.

Thankfully, murder crimes were something of a rarity during my career, but sadly they still happened. We experienced a particularly nasty murder in Gosforth after an elderly lady who lived alone had placed an advertisement for a gardener in a local shop. Once the signed-up gardener had completed his work, there had been a disagreement over the subsequent payment. This resulted in the man brutally attacking the old woman with a hammer before running off. He left her with a broken skull, described later as being akin to a smashed boiled egg. That evening, I had a phone call from the Superintendent telling me to go to the General Hospital in Newcastle and sit with the injured lady in case she recovered sufficiently to make a statement. This I did of course, but unfortunately the victim did not regain consciousness and she died. A GBH case had quickly escalated into a murder investigation.

I gathered all the available evidence at the hospital and returned to the scene where all the officers were present. It proved to be a long but fruitless enquiry, so after a few days we had little option but to call in Scotland Yard, who were the backstop for murder investigations in those days. The crime was solved a couple of weeks later when the man responsible gave himself up at a police station in London.

I have been asked occasionally during my retirement if I have ever felt that a suspect has got away with a crime for which I thought he or she should have been convicted. This is always a tricky one and I have often tried to put things into context by understanding fully the remit in which both the police and the law courts operate. Our duty as police officers stops when all the evidence has been collected and has been before the court for the judge to deal with as appropriate under his jurisdiction. Yes, there were times when all our investigative work was undermined, in cases where the offender 'got off' – but simply, it is not up to the police to decide if the suspect is found guilty or innocent. That task falls to the jury and judge to decide.

There was one occasion which stands out from my time in Gosforth, when there was a 'known' case of rape. Despite all the evidence very heavily pointing towards a guilty verdict, it ended up with the jury announcing a verdict of not guilty implying that the girl in question had led the man on. In this instance, the crime had been recorded, all the evidence gathered, and outstanding enquiries left to a minimum. Both myself and a constable felt the 'victim' was genuine and her only issue was that she had slight learning difficulties. The woman in question was working at a camp, but on visiting Newcastle she met a motorcyclist, who subsequently spent the day with her before offering to take her back to the camp that evening on his motorbike.

On route, he stopped the bike and according to the victim, had unconsented and unprotected sexual intercourse with her. She managed to escape and ran in stocking feet to a nearby farm whereupon the police were informed. Meanwhile, the offender had disappeared on his bike, the victim's handbag still inside the sidecar.

We interviewed the girl, and after making several enquiries we eventually found the motorcyclist, the motorbike with sidecar and her handbag still inside. Not surprisingly he said she'd been a willing party, whilst in truth, she was just too 'simple' to tell lies. Unfortunately, on her petticoat there were signs of old, semen stains. The counsel had played heavily on this and said she was a girl of loose morals. The reality was that her mother had bought the item from a second-hand shop but

only partially washed it in cold water which had not fully erad-
icated the stains. Unfortunately, the jury believed she was a girl
of loose morals and the offender was 'let off'.

In my mind he was a very lucky man and worse still, he was
a rapist at large in the community, whilst his victim had to live
with the guilt of having supposedly made up rape stories. On
this occasion, I didn't agree, but it was not my place to disagree,
I just had to get on with carrying out my duty.

From a personal development point of view, my time at
Gosforth added a new dimension to my career. I was now
responsible for other officers and their welfare. Male officers
had always had living quarters, whilst female officers had always
had digs with a landlady. I was able to begin the programme
of opening and furnishing a house for the women officers to
live in which improved the equality between both female and
male officers. There were of course still major inequalities at
large, not least of all the unequal level of pay, with the men still
earning significantly more than their female counterparts.

The female officers were often called upon to carry out plain-
clothes observations in a working men's club at a dance hall
where there was a secret loft based above the lady's cloakrooms.
On occasions we used to observe the dance hall and cloakrooms
directly from this attic location, and as a result resolved many
cases of handbag and purse theft. There were also times when
we were heavily distracted by some of the interesting conversations from the cloakroom below! Through our investigative
studies here, we did however succeed in uncovering a case of
intoxicating liquor being sold without a licence. As a result

of my involvement, I received a commendation by the Chief Constable for the unobtrusive and intelligent way I carried out my duties! That was high praise indeed from a senior officer, which did no harm in keeping me motivated in the tasks I was undertaking.

My time in Gosforth saw a second incident involving a man exposing himself, and as in Scarborough, my colleague and I had been keeping observations, this time at a tennis club. The incident happened over a weekend when we were 'silently observing' the situation. During our game, I noticed our suspect acting a little unusually by the fence, so I called my colleague over and my intuition told me he was building up to 'flash' at us. True to form he moved behind the building and proceeded to expose himself.

He was definitely caught off guard, as I'm sure the last thing he expected was for us to dash outside the tennis court to try to catch him. If he'd realised that I was a police sergeant, he would probably not have done this in the first place! We had a tussle with him using tennis rackets for protection and to keep him under control, which enabled us to catch hold of him before taking him to a Roman Catholic church nearby. Here, the kindly Catholic Father called for a police car, have him arrested and taken away. Remember we were still operating without radios and had to rely solely on the use of landlines. A far cry from today, but also another example of how working together in the community is an effective way to fight crime.

I remained keen to promote my own career and always took the opportunity to learn from new experiences and to take control whenever possible. On many occasions, if there was no male sergeant on duty, I would brief the team on their shift work before duty commenced. Never once was any resentment shown by the male officers as we worked very well as a team, with each of us bringing our own strengths.

Towards the end of 1959 my Chief Constable visited the station and asked me if I would like to attend the Police College. He didn't have to wait long for my reply as this was one of my pre-determined goals and I was delighted to be given the opportunity to attend. The six-month course began in January 1960 and was designed for newly promoted inspectors; sergeants qualified for promotion to inspector; and those considered suitable for promotion to this rank. This presented a real opportunity for me to take great steps towards fulfilling my career ambitions.

CHAPTER 7

MIDDLESBROUGH
TRAINING AND PROMOTION

It was an exciting time for me. Whilst still officially employed as Sergeant at Gosforth Police Station, I took my next step towards promotion. Along with two other officers from Northumberland, I travelled to the Police College at Ryton-on-Dunsmore in Warwickshire. The Police College was also home to the National Police library, so there was a wealth of information at our disposal for reference and study.

As it transpired, my group was the last full course to be held at Ryton before the college moved to Bramshill House in Hook, Hampshire. The principal police training college stayed at Bramshill House for 50 years until it went full circle and returned to Ryton in 2012.

There were 150 officers on the course, which included several overseas students, mainly from Commonwealth countries in Africa, but also a few from Hong Kong. There were three women, of which I was one! I imagine just for the purpose of keeping the numbers symmetrical, one female officer was allocated into each of the three different department groups of 50. The departments comprised of Criminal Law, Police Procedure and Liberal Studies, with each element of the course lasting two months. To help the learning process, each department was further sub-divided into groups of roughly 12 people along with a Director of Studies.

There was absolutely no distinction or privilege given to me or the other two female officers. It was a huge comfort to me to feel fully accepted as an officer first, who just so happened to also be a woman. I found the whole course thoroughly stimulating and hugely enjoyable and loved hearing the experiences of others from around the country and, indeed, other parts of the world.

The course itself was clearly preparing us, the mature students, with information and knowledge with which to propel us to the next stage of our careers. It was by no means all technical police-based learning, although the key legal principles, all sorts of formal investigative and arrest procedures and crime-exploration techniques were high on the agenda. Alongside this and mainly through our liberal studies, we also learned some of the finer social etiquette requirements. This equipped us to handle ourselves in many different social situations which we could face in the years to come.

To some degree, it felt a little like 'going back to school' as we familiarised ourselves with reading and discussion around humanities topics and the study of classic writers and poets such as Chaucer and Shakespeare. It was all designed to build character and in the eyes of the Inspectorate at the time, to develop police leaders of the right calibre, who had demonstrated themselves suitable for the higher ranks. Throughout the course there was continuous, rigorous and independent assessment of all of us, again designed to make sure that officers were only able to pass the course on merit.

During part of the course I was teamed up with an officer from the Commonwealth, specifically Tanganyika in Africa, (which later became Tanzania), to give a lecture to our fellow colleagues. I was researching a paper on the future of Africa, whilst he presented a document on nationalism in the continent. The idea was to work together in pairs, but it quickly became obvious that he felt his rank superior to a female colleague and expected me to provide the lion's share of the work whilst he filled in a few blanks! Without doubt, he was one of the lazier officers with whom I came into contact, whilst his arrogance portrayed him in a very sexist and racist light. He was certainly not one of my favourite fellow officers.

Since it proved very difficult to glean information from him directly, even though he was based in Africa with a broad knowledge, I had to use my initiative and found other ways of doing my research. I called a meeting of all the African students and asked them to explain their thoughts on policing in their continent, which I was able to capture and piece together into my presentation. Whilst it was rare to have been put upon by male colleagues, the incident with the Tanganyikan officer served to show me that not all higher-ranking officers were prepared to make the same effort and determination which I was prepared to give in order to provide the best service. I felt that he was looking to see what he could get out of his police role for selfish reasons whilst I very much thought of police work as a service to the community at large.

It was during my time at the College, that Miss Barbara Denis de Vitré visited. I knew she had not been well, but I was upset to see her looking poorly. In fact, it was not long after her visit that she sadly passed away. She had left an indelible mark on me, and I saw her as a remarkable woman and someone whom policewomen all over the country should be so proud of because of the pioneering work she had done on their behalf over the previous 20 or so years. Miss de Vitré was very much the person on whom I modelled myself, so in years to come when the Chief HMI appointed me to take up the role of Assistant to Chief HMI, the very role that Miss de Vitré held, I was so humbled to think that I was to follow in her footsteps.

She was a formidable lady, not necessarily in her physical presence, but in the steely, tenacious and yet courteous way she encouraged chief constables all around the country to employ female officers. Many chief constables may have been reluctant to employ women officers because they had managed for years without them. She worked her position so well, because the funds which paid for each provincial police force was made up from a 50% contribution from the local authorities, whilst the remaining 50% came from central government. For the half to be paid from Central Office, an HM Inspector was required to visit the local force and provide written positive feedback as to the activities which had been undertaken, ensuring that everything was being managed effectively and in line with any national directive at the time.

On occasion during the late 1940s, under Miss de Vitré's mandate, the forces had their grants threatened if they didn't employ any or sufficient women for their units, as per the guidelines laid down by the Home Office. She used her very powerful persuasive manner to influence the chief constables and in so doing brought the police force as a career opportunity to a growing number of women around the country. Her role should never be undervalued and for me she was certainly one of the leading lights in the story of women in Britain's police service.

Whilst at the Police College, I became aware that the borough of Middlesbrough was advertising for a woman inspector. This was of real interest as it was the next step up for me and was situated in my native north-east. It just so happened that my Chief Constable from Northumberland was visiting the college at around the time, so I asked him if he would support my application. Given the circumstances, I was a little reticent at first, especially as it was he who had nominated me to attend the course as a member of the Northumberland force, and it was also being paid for by them. I was very grateful that he treated me with great respect as an individual, and he supported my request to move because there were no similar vacancies in Northumberland, saying it was for the good of the service as a whole.

I subsequently applied for the post and along with three others, attended an interview, which ultimately resulted in me being the successful candidate to fill the position. I sometimes wondered what the interview body could see in me which made me suitable for the position. I can only think that my honest approach to any of the jobs I undertook helped put me in good stead whilst my record of attending courses whenever I could, and always giving my best in terms of enthusiasm and determination, were factors which helped my progression.

Middlesbrough was a borough police force with a separate women's department, incorporating an inspector, two sergeants and 20 constables. This was something new and very exciting for me. I had never previously worked in a women-only environment, nor in a department set aside from the men. At the end of my successful Police College training course, I reported for duty to take charge of the department, which was ultimately my new responsibility. My new role awaited me in a location where I had worked previously and in a town that I felt very closely aligned with, given my experiences when based in South Bank in the early to 1950s.

I quickly settled into my new surroundings, responsible for the women's department and reporting to the Deputy Chief Constable. I wasn't the first female to fill this position and I guess this helped me settle into the role as it wasn't new ground with an ambiguous question mark around it. I was fortunate to have the full support of my sergeants and constables and it was generally a solid and happy unit, full of women who enjoyed the hard work and camaraderie. I'd like to think that the way

I managed the team helped by utilising the key skills of each individual, giving autonomy for officers to take decisions when they should, but never shirking from taking tough decisions myself. I always led from the front in all areas by providing clear, concise and effective instructions.

It was a tough baptism in my newly appointed role as Inspector as we got involved in some serious crime cases, some of which hit national headlines. The Cannon Street riots took place in 1961, the year following my return to Middlesbrough. This incident followed the infamous Notting Hill riots seen down in London at the time. When put into context of the period, the Cannon Street riots may have been the catalyst for similar riots taking place in other towns and cities. It was racially motivated, at a time when there had been significant immigration into the country, largely from Pakistan. In some areas this caused tensions to run high, and this occasionally escalated into violence.

The Cannon Street riots typified this background. At the time Cannon Street was one of the toughest streets in the Ironmasters district of Middlesbrough. The area had built up notoriety over the years and had a reputation for harbouring arguments, drunkenness and fighting, so it will come as no surprise to learn that this particular neighbourhood was always on our radar down at the station.

It was regarded locally as one of the most deprived areas in the town and immediately conjures up a picture of squalor and decay with a gloomy, dank and oppressive atmosphere surrounding the dilapidated terraced housing. These dirty, run-down and drab conditions meant it was also very cheap. Housing and commercial properties were available at low rents, thereby attracting people with little money who were prepared to live in such conditions. Consequently, the area became a magnet for many immigrants who had arrived at the port of Middlesbrough seeking a new life. By no means were the locals all disreputable, but the street had maintained its bad reputation from previous years and so remained the epicentre of violence and unrest.

The riots were sparked against this background. I have reminded myself of the events which led up to the violence, by referring to news reports from the town's local newspaper, the *Evening Gazette* and from police journals kept from that period, which together helps illustrate exactly what ignited the violence.

Trouble was always brewing and in August 1961, it reached critical conditions. It was a warm, oppressive Friday evening when a gang of white youths went out onto the streets looking for trouble and came across a group of Asian men. After a barrage of insults, followed by bottles and objects flying, the fighting erupted and a white 18-year-old youth was mortally wounded in a knife attack. What followed was a breakout of largely uncontrolled violence as the crowd swelled to over a hundred youths congregating in Cannon Street, before they rampaged through the largely Pakistani area and smashed the recently erected 'Taj Mahal' which had been built by the immigrant population. The building, used largely as a café, was burned to the ground.

It was a frightening moment for the police officers who had tried to act as a barricade, with each policeman standing shoulder to shoulder as a line of defence between the gang of white youths and the Asian community. The mob soon turned their attention away from the Asian population and towards the police, with several violent attacks coming our way. As a result, our force suffered several casualties, including an officer with a fractured skull, another with a fractured spine and nine badly hurt requiring hospital treatment. Twelve rioters were put into custody.

There was a very tense atmosphere for a few days and on the Sunday, a crowd of well over 500 gathered on the streets. They targeted Pakistani-owned premises, smashing windows under a hail of stones and bottles. The area looked like a war zone which took several weeks to quieten down before it returned to some sense of normality. The riots received national attention and sparked other similar violent racist outbreaks over the country. It was a sad period. What it did provide from my perspective was a situation which had consolidated all of our police officers into a strong focused unit, with the female officers manning the control room whilst all the male personnel were outside on the front line and facing the violence head-on. In some respects, it provided a sense of unity and helped the police to battle our corner for the greater good of the community.

My work experiences over seven years in Middlesbrough were invaluable to my own police education as it was such a good training ground. Whilst the subject matter was sometimes very difficult to deal with, it made me more aware of the wider and harsher sectors of society, whilst giving me added drive and determination to help deal with some of the awful and tragic crimes that were taking place. Along with my women officers, I got very heavily involved in cases involving children. Many were very sad examples of a breakdown in family values and even worse, child neglect and cruelty. We certainly had to harden our senses whenever we needed to get involved in crimes of this nature.

My time at Middlesbrough allowed me to really get to grips with working with other outside agencies for the welfare of the family. I am delighted that I was able to establish a very good working relationship with the likes of the Children's Department, the NSPCC and the probation service, and together our collaboration of ideas helped unite us in the battle to reduce social and domestically depraved situations. We discovered many cases of neglect which were very hard on our emotions, despite all our training and experiences to date. There are several sad instances which stand out in my recollections.

We received a call at the station from a worried neighbour who was concerned that she heard crying coming from a nearby house. We arrived at the address and after knocking on the door without reply, we forced entry to find a little boy of four years old in wellington boots and a T-shirt, cowering in the cold under the stairs. The house was empty and had been for four days, except for this little lad who had been left alone to fend for himself without food or heating. We took him into our care and gave him hot milk and sandwiches until some hours later his mother arrived at the station. It turned out that she had gone to a party which lasted for several days, during which time she hadn't paused to consider her child at home and how he might have been coping, left alone by himself. Rarely have I seen any of my fellow colleagues so distressed, angered and wanting to mete out justice, but the duty Sergeant at the station was so incensed at this mother's obvious lack of compassion towards her innocent little boy, that he had to be restrained. It was a distressing case of wilful neglect which touched many of us down at the station.

There was a very unusual case of neglect which came to our attention after an NSPCC Inspector asked me to accompany him to a house on the outskirts of Middlesbrough. He had received an anonymous letter saying there were children living there who were being neglected by their parents. We arrived at the house and went inside to see a well presented, clean and seemingly comfortable home. We spoke to the woman and asked about her children and we were subsequently introduced to two young infants who appeared healthy, well-fed and well looked after. It was only after further in-depth questioning that the woman finally revealed there were two more children upstairs. We followed her upstairs into a small unfurnished room and were horrified to see two little children sitting on a dirty old mattress which was covered in human waste and bits of stale bread crust. The undernourished children were effectively isolated as prisoners in this solitary room and not allowed to leave its confines.

Further enquiries revealed that these two children were one from the mother's previous relationship and one from the father's prior marriage, whilst the two bright and cared for children in the house were of the couple's own union. It was quite unbelievable that four children lived in that house, with two enjoying a happy, healthy upbringing whilst their half-siblings were confined to a tragic and very unhappy existence. The parents were quite rightly prosecuted, and the children taken into care.

On a lighter side, we started receiving anonymous calls, normally on a Saturday evening, reporting that children were being left alone at one particular address. We visited and remained with the children until their parents returned, whereupon they were warned about the dangers of leaving children home unattended. When this happened for a third time, we realised that it was in fact the parents making the calls themselves, knowing they would have free babysitting from their generous police station until their return home! We soon put a stop to that.

We also had to deal with the administration of non-accidental injuries to children. This was a problematic area of work as it was often very difficult to determine who had caused the injury: it may have been the mother who dealt the blow but it could have been the father who had driven her to it with abusive threats and violent acts towards her. There were many cases sadly, of abuse dished out to children by their parents, which in itself became a vicious circle as there has been sufficient evidence over the years to prove that a battered child is more likely to grow up and batter his or her own children. Non-accidental injuries to children became one of my specialist areas of study and during my time in the north-east, and when I began working in Northumberland, I worked closely with a local paediatrician, Christine Cooper, and we often studied cases together. Later in life when I was working at the Home Office, I was called to give evidence of some of these cases at Select Committees in the House of Commons.

We maintained a strong presence out patrolling the streets, spending time in the dance halls and in the leisure parks, talking with the younger generation and continuing to build dialogue wherever possible. I regularly gave talks to outside organisations on the work being undertaken by our women police officers and we welcomed members of the public to our women's only department office: a small terraced house in Dunning Street, opposite the Town Hall. Many domestic issues were discussed here as women who were suffering domestic disputes could come for advice and be offered help if it were needed.

I occasionally visited the local schools at the end of term prize-giving and sometimes gave an address at assemblies. On one occasion I spoke to the girls about loyalty and during my address, I mentioned misguided loyalty. The next day the headlines in the local paper read 'Senior Police Officer says, "To split on a friend might help"'. This was picked up by the national press and as a result I received a great number of letters from around the country, accusing me of trying to breed a race of traitorous quislings! How times change!

It was around this time that promiscuity was a worry, especially among schoolgirls as young as 12 or 13, when some of them saw short-term misguided benefits from getting involved in prostitution. As part of our role, we regularly spoke with the local prostitutes, whether they were in custody or in their local public houses, notably the Captain Cook or the Robin Hood. As I had found out during my time in South Bank, they really were excellent informants, particularly when young girls went missing. We solved many cases of 'missing persons' because of the information gleaned from the prostitutes: often I received an anonymous phone call reporting that young girls had moved onto 'her' patch or were on the vessels at the docks. Admittedly, it was in their interests to have schoolgirls taken away and out of their trade, as they were regarded as young competition who often 'did "it" for just a bar of chocolate!' That was the sad truth of it unfortunately.

Middlesbrough had a large dockyard which was a regular attraction for some prostitutes, and we also realised it tempted several schoolgirls who absconded from school or remand home or simply ran away from home. The prostitutes gave us vital information, which enabled us to carry out our work and retrieve these misguided youngsters. There were occasions when we had to go down to the boats and board the vessels in search of missing girls, and this sometimes led to difficult situations in actually getting onto the boats themselves.

On one occasion, I recall taking a male and a female police officer with me and on arrival noticing that the only way onto the boat was up rope ladders on the side of the vessel. Not being very fond of heights, I was reluctant to climb, but I really had to lead the way. Gingerly I began the ascent. You may imagine the whistles coming from some of the sailors on the ship as well as some of the prostitutes who thought it rather hilarious that I had to clamber up the ladder in order to search the ship. Meanwhile, I was very aware that I was clambering up in a skirt, as trousers were not yet part of the women police officers' wardrobe. I no doubt caused merriment to the men on the docks below whilst giving them a good eyeful! The female PC could not follow, and it was with some reluctance that my male officer did. In fact, when we returned to the station, he admitted that he would not have been able to go on board if I hadn't led the way!

It wasn't uncommon to find up to 20 girls still in their school uniforms, who had absconded from school and gone to say goodbye to the sailors they had got to know in the previous days. On one occasion, we brought a group of schoolgirls who had just been taken from the ships at the docks, back to the police station at around 9am. We were noticed by the Chief Constable who said it was rather early for a school education visit. He didn't know at the time that the schoolgirls had just experienced a very different sort of education!

During the Sixties, the immigrant population continued to grow in Middlesbrough with an increasing number of men occupying the terraced houses in and around Cannon Street. Every room in these houses was furnished with a bed and as the men worked shifts, the beds were often occupied all the time. Unfortunately, these houses were a haven for girls missing from home or absconders from care or approved schools, as they were able to spend much time with these men.

In many respects, the youngsters were being groomed and we at the police station were desperate to get it under control and consequently acted whenever we could. I often visited the area with a couple of policewomen, calling on houses to check on missing girls. The occupants became aware of our presence and as soon as we arrived, one of the men would run or cycle around to other houses to warn of our coming. When they had telephones installed it became more difficult to introduce an element of surprise into our visits, but of course we persevered.

On one occasion I decided that a couple of my ladies would accompany me and call unannounced on some of the houses in Church Street, which were known to have previously welcomed young girls into their rooms. We were following up on cases of missing girls who had recently run away from home and were keen to find any news of their whereabouts. We knocked on the door of the first house, but no one came, so we knocked again but still received no answer. We were sure there were people in the house, so I opened the letterbox flap and peeked inside to see if I could see movement. I fell backwards in surprise as a startled pair of brown eyes stared back at me. I heard a similar surprised shriek coming from the house as well, as he too was caught off guard when my own wide-open eyes had startled him as much as he had startled me! True to form, the inhabitants had been overly cautious but only because they had young stowaways being groomed in their homes. We kept them under very close surveillance.

One young 13-year-old girl was brought to the station by her mother because she had fallen pregnant and had clearly been involved in illegal sexual activity. On being interviewed she alleged that the father was an Asian man, but when he was identified he denied even knowing the girl, let alone that he could be the father of her unborn child. We believed she was telling the truth, so we kept a close eye on the youth's whereabouts and activity. Sure enough, some weeks later we were in the police box next to the telephone kiosk when the suspect came out looking very happy and exclaiming that he had a son. He was arrested and charged with the offence of having unlawful sex with an underage girl and deservedly received a custodial sentence. It was always very pleasing and a massive relief to hear when offenders were found guilty and taken off the streets to spend time in prison, where they would hopefully reform themselves into becoming socially acceptable human beings.

Sometimes girls absconded from home simply because, rightly or wrongly, they felt unwanted and unloved and wanted to find some companionship with someone who showed them some affection. A compassionate story springs to mind: we found a young teenage girl who was 14 or 15 and had suddenly and very unusually left home and had gone missing for a couple of days. When we discovered her later, thankfully little worse for her experience, her first question to me, was: 'Did me mam report me missing?' When we told her that her mum had been very upset after her disappearance the young girl changed her attitude completely, as she realised that her parents really did care about her. In retrospect, a few more kind words spoken by the parents to their daughter at home would probably have prevented her from ever wanting to leave in the first place.

On a different subject, one of the biggest sporting spectacles in England's history occurred during my time serving in Middlesbrough. 1966 marked the occasion of football's global centrepiece – the FIFA World Cup. Whilst it is well known that England won the famous trophy that year at Wembley Stadium, what is less known is that Middlesbrough Football Club's stadium, Ayresome Park, was one of only eight grounds used to hold the World Cup group stage matches in England. The Boro, as the local team were known, had not enjoyed the best of seasons and had been relegated to the third division. As such they were the only club whose ground was featured in the World Cup not to be playing in the country's top two divisions. That really epitomised the high esteem in which the club and its well-manicured and maintained football surface was held by the English Football Association. In the northeast groups section, the international teams which played in Middlesbrough included Italy, Russia, Chile and the real minnows of the competition, North Korea.

At the police station, we were very much aware that the eyes of the world were on the town and the country in general and we were very keen that the tournament passed without incident, with only positive publicity surrounding the town's contribution to the event. Looking back, there was very little extra surveillance needed to look after supporters who visited from overseas and from other parts of the country. In fact, my memories simply revolve around walking up and down the terraces and in between the rows of seats at the stadium, making sure that the ground was empty of any unusual packages. I must have dreamt about lifting red wooden seats for nights on end! As things turned out, Middlesbrough and Ayresome Park witnessed one of the biggest upsets ever known in world football and will be forever remembered in the history books as the ground that saw North Korea humble the giants of world football, Italy, by winning one goal to nil!

My involvement in sporting events was relatively minimal throughout my career, although I do recall being scheduled to attend a meeting in Sunderland during May 1973. Coincidentally, the timing clashed with the Sunderland football team parading their recently won FA Cup through the town after their giant-killing victory over Leeds United at Wembley Stadium. It proved to be one of the few occasions when our meeting was left unattended in favour of joining all the spectators enjoying the team's historic victory procession travelling on an open-top bus through the town. We may have had some explaining to do about the missed meeting, but it was worth it!

My only other occasions of being on duty at sporting events were during cricket and tennis matches in Scarborough, in the North Riding. There, I was fortunate enough to meet the late, great Yorkshire fast bowler Fred Trueman, although my lasting memory was less about his prowess as a cricketer and more about his loud, abrasive and rather colourful vocabulary!

My time in Middlesbrough was an excellent learning curve. It provided a very broad outlook on life in a way that the county forces I had previously been employed within could never have given me. However, my life in the police force to date told me that I needed to keep changing roles every five or six years. I needed to face fresh, new challenges; stay thirsty for greater responsibility; and gain a broader knowledge of the police service. I felt ready for my next step, so when the opportunity arose for me to return to Northumberland, I accepted the challenge and applied for the position of Chief Inspector.

CHAPTER 8

NORTHUMBERLAND
A COMPLETELY NEW ROLE

My application to become Chief Inspector proved successful and I made my transition northwards to Northumberland on 8th April 1967. I was to meet a quite different set of challenges than I had previously faced in my career. This was a big move for me, which had not seemed at all possible 17 years previously. I remember feeling quite positive following my second interview for the role, especially when the Assistant Chief Constable told me that I had given a very good interview. I saw him a little later that day and he said again that I'd done really well. Despite this, I was kept hanging for a day or two – he didn't let on that I had got the job.

My new job was much more of a managerial role than I had previously experienced, looking after and supporting the force of 35 policewomen stationed across several locations in the county. Of course, this involved spending time at different stations, helping to propose and implement our key strategies for that specific locality whilst maintaining focus on the entire region. My priority was less about me carrying out specific daily duties and more about setting the key objectives for all the women officers and looking after their well-being and motivations for the job.

The number of women officers in the new force increased significantly so my time spent on recruitment and training also increased. I began to think much more clearly about the duties performed by my officers and what was expected of them. This was also a prerequisite for potential new officers coming into the police, which forced me to think long and hard about the key characteristics of new recruits, whilst also looking for any early signs of potential for advancement to the level of inspector or above.

At the start of the process of finding a suitable potential new female police officer, there were first some obvious physical conditions which needed to be met – she had to be at least five feet four inches, physically fit with good eyesight and of an age which also met the regulations (ranging from 18 to 20 during my time in the force). From an educational perspective, an entrance exam needed to be taken (or an equivalent academic qualification attained), as well as a physical exam and if both were passed, there followed an interview process for us to be able to pick the wheat from the chaff.

Wherever possible, I always preferred interviews for any candidate to take place in their own homes and certainly by a female inspector. This provided a more relaxed atmosphere for the candidate so she could be more natural and less reserved about what she may or may not want to say. It also provided a better picture of herself and her family life. This was followed by a second interview at the station, which again, always included a female officer, and provided greater opportunities for questions to be asked by both parties to find out a little more about each other. This process really helped us see if the candidate had the stamina for the role and if they were able to leave a strong positive impression.

During the interview process, I always felt it important to stress the areas of the job which could be seen as disadvantageous, so the candidate knew exactly what they were potentially signing up to; the shift work; working Sundays; restricted time off; joining a profession as a way of life not a normal nine to five job; and to always be prepared to forego certain things in order to finish a job. At the same time, I looked for the successful candidate to be able to get on with people from across the social spectrum and to have a sense of humour, or even better, perhaps a slightly warped sense of humour! These attributes would help any new recruits (female or male) communicate effectively with different types of people from different walks of life.

Any new officer was on probation for a two-year period and reported on every three months to measure their individual progress against key set objectives. During this time, there was the opportunity for either the police or the recruit to call a halt to their police career if things had not measured up as expected.

The rejection rate was quite high and slightly higher for women than for men. The biggest issue was recruits not having done their background research on what the job entailed or not fully understanding what was involved in the role. There were several examples of women looking to join the force as an officer because they thought the uniform was smart and it would make them look professional, without having given any thought to what the role actually entailed!

New recruits were monitored throughout their career, which allowed us to build up a profile of the key characteristics required for an officer with the ability to progress through the ranks, to the level of inspector or beyond. As well as showing leadership, vision and directional qualities, promotable officers are: clear and logical thinkers; able to communicate and express these ideas clearly and concisely to people from across the social spectrum; able to lead from the front with courage, both physical and moral; resourceful and can adapt to situations whilst remaining fair-minded and impartial. They take pride in doing a job for pride's sake and not always for reward; have integrity, have high standards of honesty and are wholly trustworthy; show good manners, respect, consideration and empathy towards others; are ultimately loyal and dedicated to the police service.

I've always looked back with fondness at recruits whom I have seen come into the force and then move up through the ranks by showing these kinds of strong and positive character traits and of course, by being very good at their job. It's so refreshing to see a new young recruit develop in their role with a positive frame of mind and with the support of strong counselling, guidance and training. I hope that somewhere along the way, I have helped many women carve out strong careers for themselves in the police force.

In an attempt to paint a realistic picture of the required officer personality strengths and character traits, I have found my own assessment document from 1968. This was required in advance of attending a course suitable for Chief Inspectors who were looking for promotion to the rank of Women Chief Superintendent. It read:

Women Chief Inspector SIGSWORTH is a very cheerful and efficient officer. She is dedicated to the Police Service as a career and has ambition to progress further. She has seen service in two Counties and a Borough Force and has gained considerable experience which she is able to apply intelligently. Firm in command, she is still able to command the respect both of her experienced Sergeants and the junior policewomen. She is interested in all aspects of her work and while paying due regard to the requirements of the Women's Section, she does not antagonise her male colleagues. She makes every endeavour to integrate the work of the Policewomen with that of the men.

With an ability to mix with all classes, she is presently co-operating very fully with representatives of the Social Services at all levels.

In my view Miss Sigsworth has the ability to administer a happy and efficient Women's Section and I am quite confident that she could efficiently discharge the responsibilities of a Woman Chief Superintendent. I therefore consider her to be a suitable candidate for the Intermediate Command Course.

I enjoyed visiting the different police stations and talking to the female officers and with their divisional commanders about their duties and performance. It was a new experience for me to receive phone calls from different chief superintendents giving me an update on my women officers, perhaps saying that one had done an excellent job, or maybe another had difficulties when faced with a particular challenge. Whatever the discussion, we always had an excellent rapport and I'm pleased to say that I got on with my male colleagues extremely well, whilst they treated me with the same courtesy, respect and humour.

There was only one occasion which springs to mind when I felt a little aggrieved at being singled out as a woman in a man's world. It occurred following an evening dinner which I attended as the only female present, and which included some high-ranking community officials as well as press and of course, senior members of the police. After the meal had finished and port and brandy were poured, my Chief Constable, who was rather 'old school' in outlook, looked at me and gave me an obvious nod, indicating that it was time to leave the room, so the gents could enjoy a drink along with their cigars. I appreciate this was something of a tradition, but I really felt quite awkward and wasn't entirely sure what to do next. I left the room and ended up sitting outside chatting with the cleaners. I imagine I could have made a fuss, and possibly with some justification, but I always tried to keep a balanced approach and as such was able to make progress in an acceptable way.

That's not to say I always kept quiet if I felt my seniors were out of order. There were times when it was important to let people know the limits of my tolerance. Throughout my career, I have been exposed to some extremely foul language but there were also times when I have felt it completely unnecessary to drop standards to such a level, particularly among colleagues. I remember one instance in Northumberland, when an Assistant Chief Constable kept using offensive language in a meeting when it really was totally unnecessary. Since the bad language continued unabated, I took a stance and walked out of the room, simply refusing to listen to the abusive language any longer. It hit the mark. The Assistant Chief Constable apologised to me and I asked that he showed the same courtesy to other people involved in the meeting. In fairness he did, and never again resorted to using such unnecessary language in any meeting I had with him. That was respectful and courteous of him.

My office was at the headquarters in Morpeth and later at Ashington, whilst I recruited throughout the county and liaised with divisional commanders at their respective stations. During this time there were several amalgamations of police forces throughout the country, all part of the police restructuring programme. One in particular significantly affected the north-east area. In 1969 the Northumberland County Constabulary combined with Newcastle Upon Tyne Borough Police and Tynemouth Borough Police, more than doubling its size and strength and in so doing, became known as the Northumberland Constabulary.

This amalgamation was a major task, which required a different set of skills in helping to manage the process. I certainly had to broaden my knowledge as I worked alongside fellow senior officers to fathom out the logistics for uniting three different and autonomous forces which had each previously run under different working methods, practices and procedures.

To break down any barriers across the amalgamated forces, I set up a new group which included different members from across the amalgamated forces and different social agencies. We met monthly for strategic planning purposes and occasionally had weekends away at different events or listened to different speakers at universities. These were designed as ways of helping to build bridges and trust across the force and social agencies, and introduce a standardisation across the stations under the new amalgamated structure. As with many things, the crux of finalising a strong and efficient amalgamation largely revolved around firm and effective communication at all levels, from attending all the associated strategic planning meetings to discussing the finer detail with officers across the stations.

I was reminded of how small the world really is, when on one occasion I was introduced to a Director of Social Services by the Chief Constable. When he turned around, the man I was looking at turned out to be an old school friend from when I was at Easingwold Grammar School nearly 40 years previously! We both looked shocked as the chances of meeting an old classmate from four decades ago to discuss a major policy matter for the county must have been quite low. A small world indeed.

Throughout this rather tough period involving lots of decision-making, when there were many issues under review, I found that I was talking to myself more than usual. Someone noticed and commented to me on this, and I was able to rationalise by saying many fellow officers had families to go home to and 'download' their day, providing an outlet for their feelings and challenges they were facing. As I was living alone, with no partner, I had got into the habit of talking through the pros and cons of things with Him 'upstairs'. My faith really helped me and often if I was 'talking' through my challenges at home in the evening, when I awoke the following morning I would have greater clarity and a stronger vision for what I was looking to achieve. It was a comforting way to get my head around important issues... and it worked for me.

This new police structure was part of the revolution of the provincial police forces nationwide and was necessary to provide a more efficient and effective police network through-out the country. The respective amalgamations ensured greater compatibility and a more consistent framework in which each force operated, whilst at the same time, improved the public perception of the police as a professional organisation.

The amalgamation of the forces also meant that the senior women's responsibilities grew accordingly, and as a result, a new position of Superintendent was created to take control of the growing number of female officers. I can vividly recall that the interview process was very tough, as I had very close competition from another police chief inspector, who was already working at the Newcastle Police Station and clearly also looking for her next promotion.

Ultimately, I was handed the job, and perhaps only naturally there was some initial coldness from my colleague whom I had just beaten to the role. This only added to my pressures, having joined a new force and in a new position which was a significant step up from my previous roles. My personnel responsibility meant I was now in charge of all the women officers in the Northumberland force, stationed throughout the whole county and I could ill afford to have potential difficulties with my most senior fellow female colleagues in the force. I needed to nip in the bud any initial unfriendliness or frostiness towards me as I was determined to have a strong united team, fighting on the same front and working towards the same goals.

Around the same time, I was also selected to attend the Intermediate Command Course at the Police College, which I mentioned earlier in the chapter, along with 27 men and one other woman. It was rather unfortunate timing that as soon as I had been promoted to superintendent – the first woman to reach that rank in the region – I had to leave and attend the three-month course. The officer whom I had narrowly beaten was chief inspector, but almost immediately had to grasp the mettle and in my absence take on the role of acting superintendent. It was to her credit that she dealt with the situation positively and we were able to move forward without complications upon my return.

How was I able to overcome any seeming hostility towards me? Well, I simply spoke to my colleague in the way that I would have wanted her to speak to me if the roles had been reversed – with honesty and humility. I explained how much I valued her efforts and experience in this police district and was looking forward to receiving her help and support, under my management, to build a strong women's unit here in the north-east of England. If this was something she really couldn't believe in, that would be very sad.

This had been my approach during my whole working life, so why be different now? That simple philosophy has served me well – to have straightforward, effective communication showing politeness but firmness, and all the time having utmost respect for other people. As things transpired, she proved to be a very good chief inspector and ultimately, my right-hand 'man' and we ended up working very well together for several years. Central to this was our agreement that any differences between us would be kept to the confines of my office for discussion, so that we always showed a united front to the rest of the department.

As for the three-month course, it proved very informative and an extremely worthwhile experience which helped me in the challenges that faced me on my return to Northumberland and the subsequent amalgamation of forces.

Over the course of the next few months, the challenges were met head-on, and we steadily made progress in uniting the three previous autonomous bodies into a single fully resourced unit. It was by no means plain sailing and we faced a certain amount of acrimony from some personnel, not just in the service but also with outside agencies. However, with patience, endurance and perseverance, our united efforts paid off and the Northumberland Constabulary was born.

This meant we were well prepared for the next logistical challenge, which was a further continuation of the restructuring programme within the provincial police forces. In 1974, as a result of the local government boundaries being revised, the composition of the Northumberland Constabulary changed again. This time it was merged with additional areas within the metropolitan county of Tyne and Wear (including Sunderland and the northern part of the Durham Constabulary) to become one of the nation's largest police forces, the Northumbria Constabulary.

During this period, I maintained my close relationship with child support groups, notably the NSPCC, children's departments, social services and paediatricians as my special interest of study was still non-accidental injury to children. The trust and relationships built in this period proved invaluable in later years at the Home Office, when I was able to speak from first-hand experience in front of Select Committees at the House of Commons. My group of trusted and close confidantes held many meetings with agencies across the growing Northumbria district and met regularly at the Cathedral in Newcastle, involving the clergy in discussions.

It was becoming more and more necessary to have these meetings, simply because the number of cases of what became known as 'baby battering' was increasing. This was largely as a result of significantly increased press coverage – regionally and nationally – which in turn led to a growing number of cases being reported to the Northumbria Police and across the country. It seemed to be the 'hot' topic of the period which had clearly caught the public's imagination, which in turn added pressures for the cases to be dealt with expediently and efficiently.

The numbers of incidents could have been even higher as it became increasingly apparent that many parents were taking their children to different hospitals in efforts to avoid detection. It was during these hospital visits that babies were found to have healing fractures of various kinds as a result of previous non-accidental injuries sustained. We were increasingly concerned with finding the root cause of these incidents and questioned the ability of young people to cope with the modern-day stresses of that period. It was my belief that pressures on families had grown out of social conditions in the new high-rise flats which were little more than 'filing cabinets' for people. These new estates had removed easy accessibility to nearby family, where granny lived on the corner and 'Aunt Maud' lived just up the street, and when there was always someone to run to in times of stress.

In cases where families suffered unemployment, this also contributed to more cases coming to light because of the additional stress on parents. I felt that schools could better prepare youngsters to fully understand their responsibilities in parenthood, particularly as many were marrying earlier. Our work increased as we now kept up-to-date written records of every case in the force area, but it also proved fruitful in the prevention of further suffering to children. One big difficulty in preventing this crime, despite greater awareness through publicity, was that many of the assaults did not come to light until the act had already taken place and someone spotted a bruise on a baby, which then often resulted in the discovery of healing fractures.

The number of cases remained high because of the daily pressures on young people with families and their inability, in some instances, to contend with them. We had instigated our review committees which involved agencies from across the spectrum who had interest in families, including social services, medical staff, the clergy and the NSPCC. We dealt with the problem as best as possible with the resources we had at our disposal. This remained a key area of study for me, and I was able to follow up on a national level with information gathered and associated feedback and report to Parliamentary bodies during my time at the Home Office in the latter part of my career.

One of the biggest criminal cases I was involved in during my career occurred whilst I was Chief Inspector at Northumberland in 1968, just prior to the amalgamation with Newcastle City Police. It involved an awful case of child abuse which ultimately resulted in child murder. Mary Bell appeared for trial at the Assize Court in Newcastle and I was responsible for ensuring she was in safe keeping whilst the court was in process. Much has been written about the case, but in brief, it involved the death by strangulation of two young boys, aged three and four, by Mary Bell, who was only ten years old at the time. I spent a considerable amount of time with her during the court sessions, and she showed herself to be a bright young girl, always following the evidence throughout whilst making observations in the waiting room.

The case was reported upon nationally and resulted in Mary being convicted of manslaughter on the grounds of diminished responsibility in December 1968, for the deaths of these two toddlers. Reports from that period say that the jury took their lead from the diagnosis offered by the court-appointed psychiatrists who described her as displaying 'classic symptoms of psychopathy'. Following the judge's ruling that she still posed a 'very grave risk to other children' and was considered dangerous, she was sent to prison for an indeterminate period. Her incarceration ended up being around 12 years before her release in 1980 when she was also granted anonymity.

Many years after her trial, an account was made by Mary Bell herself, that she had been subject to physical abuse at the hands of her prostitute mother which included the forced taking of pills and having 'accidental' falls out of a window. She also confirmed that she had been subject to sexual abuse by her mother's clients from the age of four. As a result of this physical abuse, Mary had suffered brain damage to her prefrontal cortex, an area associated with voluntary movements and decision-making.

It was a tragic case and highlighted once more the evidence that youngsters who suffered abuse were very likely to abuse others later in life. In Mary Bell's case this involved killing two innocent little boys whilst she was still merely a child herself, albeit an abused child who had witnessed countless horrors already. One wonders whether the crime would have been committed if Mary Bell had not, herself, been subjected to severe and lengthy abuse during her childhood in her own home and at the hands of her own mother.

During my time as Superintendent, my level of responsibility grew in line with the huge increase in geographical area, and many diverse communities which the Northumbria Police now covered. My learning curve steepened, and my confidence grew as I often had to front the operation by submitting and communicating reports and updating the press on various cases which were under review and had yet to be solved. My dealings with outside agencies increased enormously, as it was very clear to me that a joint approach when dealing with challenging issues was much more fruitful. This meant the police could co-operate with relevant professional bodies who were very closely aligned with our own specific challenges.

I was responsible for the welfare of women officers which included regularly revamping their specialist training for when they were tasked with specific duties. I relied heavily on my supervisory officers to keep the training worthwhile and relevant.

I had always tried to impress upon my officers the importance of getting involved in activities within the police and the community but separate to their normal official police duties. A range of extra-curricular activities added colour and variety to my everyday police role. My previously mentioned position as manager of the former St Hilda's approved school at Gosforth was an interesting distraction and one which was closely aligned with my official police work. I also chaired the management committee of the Home for Alcoholics in Newcastle which again served as a social community role. Throughout my time in the force, I was a member of St John Ambulance and often rallied with our team, and we won several cups at regional and national competitions.

Throughout the 1970s there was considerable political debate regarding the Sex Discrimination Act and more importantly for the police, the challenging question of whether there should be any discrimination between male and female police officers. The 1970 Equal Pay Act was enforced by the police service on 1st September 1974 (employers had until December 1975 to comply) and from that day it was agreed women would receive equal pay for work of equal value. Not before time in my view! This had been my biggest gripe as there is no reason why there should ever have been inequality in work-related pay. However, the Sex Discrimination Act was more complex and specifically so for the police, in which there was such a wide range of services. This led to several long debates and differences of opinion.

It was originally intended that police officers should be excluded from the section dealing with discrimination in employment. I felt there were several main reasons behind this: most notably, that although women police were recruited into the service to provide the same service as the policemen, they also fulfilled a specialist role and would continue to be needed. Secondly, outside the Metropolitan Police area, it was accepted that there was a need for an establishment of 5% women in every force to carry out the duties required to be done by women. Additionally, women were accepted into the service at the minimum height of five feet four inches, so if they were included in the Act some chief constables might have decided women should reach the same minimum height requirements as the male officers – a force of near 'Amazonian' women. Qualifications for entry were identical for men and women, apart from height restrictions.

I agreed that police officers should be excluded from the Sex Discrimination Act and that separate establishments for women should be preserved. I also felt the Rank Structure Report adequately catered for progress by women and provided these recommendations were adhered to, then I foresaw no problems. Any law which could not be enforced was, in my mind, a bad law and I felt that if the police service was included in the Act it would be impossible and certainly impracticable to enforce anti-discrimination law within the service. Men and women were recruited for special qualities and although many of the duties were interchangeable, some were not and for this reason both sexes should be necessarily employed. It was recognised in the police service that there were certain posts not suitable for women officers because of the physical demands attached to them – this would have been discrimination from the very outset thereby creating difficulties for the future.

However, as things transpired through parliamentary debate, it soon became clear that the police service would be included in any legislation governing equal opportunities. Separate establishments for men and women in police forces would cease to exist, as indeed would separate career structures. In September 1974 I was asked to join a sub-committee to look at the duties of women police in a future which would effectively make it illegal to discriminate between the roles played by male and female officers.

My overriding concern was that the police service should always have a few women officers available to deal with the work which a woman needed to do for reasons of propriety, for example, searching women, interviewing women and children in sexual cases, dealing with women prisoners where there were no female matrons. The specialist duties performed by women officers would always be present and to complete these satisfactorily and efficiently, women officers would require additional training instruction during their probationary period. I proposed that a short course of three days held at the Force Training Department would satisfy this need.

Once the separate career structure for women police disappeared when the new Act became law, then women would be considered for promotion alongside men. I felt it important that women should be given opportunities to equip themselves for service in all ranks, which meant they must have the opportunity to serve in all branches and across the different police departments. Above all I felt it really important that a nucleus of women in each of the divisions covering the major conurbations, should be employed on specialist duties to do women's work. The remainder would carry out general police duties, for example panda and foot patrols, manning the control room, and other duties considered necessary by the divisional commanders. In the two rural divisions, I agreed that it would be very difficult to conform to this recommendation because of lack of numbers, so women should be fully integrated into general police work and employed as police officers, firstly, using their specialist role as required.

In areas of my responsibility, I had already tried to foster integration and provide women with greater opportunities particularly in CID and the Traffic Department. However, I had real concerns that despite potentially bringing more women into the force, fewer would advance to more senior positions. This was simply because few women remained in the service beyond about their first seven years, which was roughly the time at which officers were considered 'available for promotion'.

The new Act came into effect immediately after I had left the Northumbria Police Force, and effectively meant that it was no longer possible to describe some aspects of policing as 'men's work' and other aspects as 'women's work'. The Act would go on to provide gender equality across all professions, thereby opening up many more opportunities for women, but there were certainly sound reasons as to why, initially at least, it did not help the police service prosper seamlessly in its transition into the new era.

During the time of the second amalgamation with the northern area of the Durham Constabulary, I was invited to become Staff Officer to the Assistant Inspector of Constabulary at the Home Office. I felt privileged to have been asked, but the timing wasn't great as we were in the middle of restructuring and I felt my work had not yet been completed in the Northumbria Force.

It was another year before I was invited again, and by then, the new Northumbria Constabulary had been created and was in safe hands. I took the opportunity to move out of my comfort zone and take my career on to the next stage. I decided to move away from my native north-east and made the rather daunting journey south to London, whereupon I was promoted to the same rank as that of a Chief Superintendent on New Year's Day 1976. I said 'Goodbye' to the fresh air of Northumberland and 'Hello' to the hustle and bustle of London and my new home, appropriately named the Home Office.

CHAPTER 9

LONDON
TO THE HEART
OF POWER

A new year and a new dawn. That's what January 1st 1976 heralded for me and to the country at large. On a personal level, it was my first day serving as Staff Officer to Nora Hughes, the Assistant Inspector of Constabulary, as I joined company with the staff of the Police Inspectorate at the Home Office. On a broader level, it was the first day in which the Sex Discrimination Act came into force and in so doing affected every working woman in the country.

Moving to the south of England was a big change when my entire life had been previously spent in my native north-east. Fortunately, I was able to keep my house in Morpeth, and whilst in London lived with my dear sister, May, in Maidenhead. I felt comfortable living in the leafy suburbs of this town in the Royal County of Berkshire, which was very nicely situated next to the River Thames and about 25 miles from London, so well within the commuting belt.

The different environment really struck home on my first day commuting by train into London. I noticed rows of men standing on the railway platform, hiding their heads behind newspapers or looking aimlessly into the sky or down at the ground, with little attention given to anyone else. My efforts at 'Good morning' were largely met with stunned silence apart from a few surprised nods, such was the difference in standard courtesy to which I had been accustomed. I persisted, and over the coming weeks and months got to know several commuters by sight. On the train one day, I recognised and spoke to a fellow commuter, whom I knew from church. He introduced me to some of his friends as 'Aunty Phyllis!' This was the only name he knew me by, as it is how I was known at church. It certainly broke the ice!

In our small department, there were three members of staff responsible to the Chief Inspector of Constabulary, notably an Assistant Inspector, a Staff Officer and a Personal Assistant. The Assistant Inspector and the Staff Officer had responsibility for visiting police forces in England and Wales.

We attended meetings with staff in the Home Office Police Department on any matters relevant to women or children, and gave evidence at the House of Commons' Select Committees. This was a complete change of role, but I felt comfortable because of the extensive practical knowledge and experience gained in the 25 years prior to my appointment.

But still an intrinsic part of my role was to see that my ladies in blue from around the country were happy with their lot. This very much included making sure that following the Sex Discrimination Act, they really were getting equal opportunities and taking full advantage of what was available to them. Sadly, my time at each station was often limited to only a single day as retirements meant that I was doing a job that had previously been shared.

Visiting police forces around the country was quite challenging at first, as I found myself looking into a service I had worked for, for many years, but one that was changing with the times. The introduction of the Sex Discrimination Act saw the cessation of the Women Police Departments. They simply did not exist any longer. Separate gender-specific establishments and career structures had been abolished and police officers were no longer distinguished as male or female. All police officers were exactly that... police officers.

Prior to this period, female officers had a separate rank structure within their own departments, often located in a physically separate part of the building, with their offices and changing facilities and a similarly segmented set of tasks to carry out. The Sex Discrimination Act changed all that and made it illegal to discriminate against women in education, recruitment and advertising, whilst the Employment Protection Act introduced statutory maternity promises and made it illegal to sack women who were pregnant.

I found that many women officers were resentful of our visits to their stations, whilst most chief constables were supportive and supplied us with information we requested in relation to the female officers working with them. It was important to ensure that the work and responsibilities previously carried out by women officers were considered when changes were made, and policy made clear throughout all stations in the country. Just before my retirement in 1979, 23 of the 43 forces had established some means of making this happen and provided a seamless transition of responsibilities for cases which had previously been worked by women officers.

It was a difficult time for women, but there had been a gradual integration over the years as women had been appointed in small numbers in CID, the Traffic Department and other specialist duties, including the mounted branch and dog handlers. I recall one of my officers surprising me with a request to attend a firearms training course. On discussing the matter, my officer made it clear that in the right circumstances she would have no hesitation in shooting to kill a person. The clinical severity of this sort of statement made me realise that times and attitudes were changing rapidly, and the police service was following suit.

I looked forward to hearing about different and interesting experiences whenever I visited different forces all over the country and could talk with the female officers, finding how their change in working conditions and roles they were now undertaking were affecting them and the work they were doing. The stock answer when asked about the duties they were performing was, 'The same as the men.'

It was always so important to quickly move past formalities and have a genuine conversation. I remember asking one nervous lass now treading a beat which I knew well: 'And at the end of the night shift, do you go into the bakery for a cup of tea and a toasted teacake like we used to?' Suddenly 'Ma'am from the Home Office' was one of them and discussion began to flow much more freely.

I enjoyed visiting some of the old haunts I had worked as an officer and I felt it very important to let the young officers know that many of us older women had gained huge experience doing exactly what they were doing. I wanted them to realise that we too had worked, out on the beat, alongside our male colleagues, carrying out the same duties and working the same shifts, even if we had only received 90% of the pay.

When visiting one of the more rural county forces, a young officer said her next case was one which involved anthrax, so I asked her if she knew how to proceed with the case. Witnessing the shocked expression on her face, I was able to tell her exactly how to deal with the case which had affected cattle and sheep and the likelihood of the disease reoccurring out in the field. It was obvious that the new officer had asked some of the older policemen in the county force what she should mention to the HMI (Her Majesty's Inspector) who was coming to the station. They suggested mention anthrax as the HMI wouldn't know anything about that as it was so far removed from city life!

Little did she know that my own experiences as a young constable had given me a broad insight into such cases, so I was able to surprise her with an educated and correct response to her question. I chuckled at this example because we used to do the same many years previously: trying to catch out the HMIs when they were doing their rounds. I was forever grateful to have had such a wide and varied career, which gave me the confidence to deal with many different situations and challenges.

I had served as staff officer for just over a year when the Assistant retired, and the Chief HMI came into my office and asked me to take up the position of Assistant to the Chief HMI with special responsibilities for women in the service and other matters relating to women, children and community work. I can vividly recall that feeling of surprise, elation and pride at being invited to step into the shoes previously occupied by someone I held in such high esteem, Miss Barbara Denis de Vitré.

I readily accepted and with the same undying enthusiasm took on the role, that I could now proudly say I had achieved the highest-ranking position possible for a female police officer working in the provinces. (The Inspectorate at that time did not cover the Metropolitan Force). My new role was very strategic and directional, and front facing, having to spend much time lecturing at the Police College, attending many policy meetings and representing the police at a variety of different functions.

I was a frequent visitor to the House of Commons, representing the Home Office on several issues and as such had to give presentations to several high-ranking ministers. These included Willie Whitelaw, who was Home Secretary during my time in London. Whilst giving lectures or making speeches could be a rather daunting experience, I always took comfort in knowing that some adrenalin was necessary to help keep me focused and in control of the situation. My advice to anyone needing to make an after-dinner speech or presentation is not to drink alcohol beforehand and certainly not to excess, if you want to keep in full control of proceedings. It is always important to have reference notes as well, just in case of forgetfulness or getting tongue tied!

I almost had one very bad experience when it came to preparing and making a presentation at an important high-profile event. Almost. In 1979 an international conference had been planned which revolved around my specialist subject of non-accidental injuries. I was going to play a key role. The day prior to the conference I had collated all the relevant paperwork and distribution copies and carefully arranged them into a wallet ready for the following morning. I subsequently took the Underground train on the Circle Line and headed for Paddington and the commute home. It was only when I had boarded the train, homeward bound for Maidenhead that I realised with horror that the wallet containing all the documents was no longer with me! I had left it on the Underground train. In desperation I jumped off the train at the next station, found a telephone box and promptly started ringing around the Tube stations to see if anyone had found a set of Private & Confidential papers.

You can imagine my anxiety – an international conference the following morning and I had misplaced all the necessary documents! I rang my sister to say that I would be late home because I simply had to do everything I could to discover their whereabouts. My relief was palpable when May said she had just received a message from Baker Street Station, and my documents had been handed in by a fellow commuter. It transpired that my saviour had found my clearly marked papers sticking out of the bin; they must have been placed there by another commuter who had thought them rubbish that needed throwing away. With massive relief I managed to pick up the paperwork and still arrived home a couple of hours before midnight. My blushes had been spared and I only wish I knew who had handed the papers in at the station, so I could thank them in person.

I was fortunate to have a couple of real stand-out moments towards the end of my career. During December 1978, out of the blue, I received a letter from Buckingham Palace advising me that I was going to be awarded the Queen's Police Medal for distinguished service in the New Year's Honours list. I was surprised to receive this news, yet, of course, I felt so proud at having this honour bestowed on me. I was the only woman out of the 16 officers from England and Wales to receive the honour on this occasion, and it was the epitome of what I had been progressing towards all those years previously when I was working as a clerk at the North Riding Constabulary, naively planning my future as a police constable. Little did I know back then where my ambitions would lead me... One of the hardest aspects for me was to keep this news a secret for over a month – I was so desperate to share my news with May and her husband!

In 1979 I was proudly presented to the Queen Mother representing the provinces at the Metropolitan Policewomen's

60th anniversary celebration dinner. In fact, I was the only non-Metropolitan officer in attendance at the event. We had a wonderful dinner at a hotel in the centre of London, whose name I cannot recall, and sad to say, was demolished several years ago. I remember nervously standing in line, before being presented to Her Majesty. I recall the Queen Mother saying to me, 'Miss Sigsworth, our lady who looks after all the policewomen in the provinces.' I was bursting with pride.

During my career I had a few brief forays into the world of royalty, all in the course of duty. I had met the Queen Mother fleetingly once before, at an event hosted up in Berwick, during my time in Northumberland. I was also part of the security force looking after the Queen one day when she visited Hexham. Any time I was close by, I thought she remained so lovely, always relaxed, friendly and courteous with whoever she came into contact. There were similar instances when I worked alongside the security forces for Princess Anne when she visited Washington, Tyne & Wear, in the early 1970s. All such occasions have been welcome distractions from everyday police life out in the provinces.

Finally, I was proud to be invited to the Guildhall to receive the Freedom of the City of London. It was an honorary award in recognition of my service in the police force and, as such, it really was the icing on the cake, to bring my career to a close. Subsequently, I have been able to enjoy the benefits of social events throughout my retirement, ranging from events of historical interest and dinners and receptions in historic locations, to an annual banquet with the Lord Mayor at the Guildhall and an annual service in the church of St Lawrence Jewry next to the Guildhall. These events have provided me and close friends with so much pleasure over the years and I've thoroughly enjoyed joining in with the traditions and ceremony at some wonderful social functions, including dinner at the House of Commons.

Just a few days prior to my 50th birthday at the end of October 1979, I became the last woman to serve in the Home Office Inspectorate in the role of Assistant to the Chief Inspector of Constabulary, where I had advised on all matters concerning policewomen. As a result of the Sex Discrimination Act, the last position I held was abolished as it no longer performed a direct function within the new police structure. So, it was with mixed feelings that I retired from the police service, but with some concerns that there wouldn't be a woman's voice in the Inspectorate. I had been part of the working party before the Sex Discrimination Act became law and, at the time, maintained that I didn't want the Act, the service didn't want it, but it was thrust upon us. Having said that, the service made real progress towards equal opportunities for men and women. Many forces still needed to find a way to fill the gap left by the abolition of the women's departments. I felt that the new departments needed to incorporate the work that female officers used to do, using the best qualified personnel.

I left the police service with my index-linked police pension intact, to help me enter retirement a few days before my 50th birthday. I had an open mind, masses of experience and was well equipped to continue serving society, this time in a voluntary capacity. I had boundless energy and was looking forward to the next phase of my life...

CHAPTER 10

REFLECTIONS ON MY POLICE CAREER

Early into my retirement, I reflected on my career and on the role that police were expected to cover during my period of working, dealing with individuals from the cradle to the grave. In order to do this, police officers were expected to be midwives, nursemaids, counsellors, psychiatrists, law enforcement officers, peacemakers, advisors and friends to all classes of people. It was accepted that police officers were servants of the public and by virtue of this, we had created one of the finest police services in the world, unbiased by politics, race or creed and at the time, unarmed.

As a result of increased crime in the post-war period, police had to concentrate more on law enforcement and consequently had to surrender a great deal of their social services role. Specialist agencies such as the Probation Service and the Social Services department took away from the police the more agreeable and humanitarian work we used to do. As a young policewoman I used to visit several houses on a Friday night to assist wives in their financial problems, helping them to set money aside for necessities, and, in addition, I used to visit wives whose husbands were in prison. Women police departments always collected toys at Christmas and either took them to needy families themselves or joined with the NSPCC to carry out this work. We always kept clothes in the office for babies and young children and the number of women who used to call at the office just for a talk was quite considerable – today it would be called counselling and they would be referred to social services and statutory associations who are far better equipped with more resources than we had at the police station.

We saw some withdrawal of support for and rapport with the police over the years as car ownership became more widespread and motorists seemed to think we regarded them as a potential criminal in the eyes of the law. It seemed that car drivers became more suspicious of police intentions if they had a car in their possession.

The restructuring of the police which resulted in the amalgamation of forces, certainly weakened local links with communities but improved efficiency and saw the police service emerge in a more professional role. At the end of my career, the police were probably respected more, whereas 20 or 30 years previously, the police force were more cherished as helpers in the local community.

Changes in society as a whole certainly affected the role of the police as my career developed. One of the most important was the widespread challenge to authority, particularly amongst young people, who developed a more questioning, critical attitude towards authority as a concept. I felt the police service should always try to maintain their traditional role in playing the cool, good-humoured police officer, because once we switched to overtly tougher measures we would be in severe danger of moving towards a more oppressive police force, which would likely be irreversible.

An important area of promotion was in schools, so we created closer links with them and universities to try to reduce problems. How we view ourselves as a police force has always been important, so training was always crucial and developed to take recruits as civilians and turn them into police officers. I always felt that training should be constantly improved with new techniques and assisted by modern aids, but wher- ever possible not to turn the police into an emergency service merely responding to complaints. I thought then as I do now, that to retain our status in the community, we must devote time to talking to people, to individuals, on the street. But with more specialisation introduced into the service, including traffic, CID, drugs, and special branch, it was not possible for all officers to be 'Jack of all trades' and a friend to all.

As a service we were often reticent to dress the 'shop window' of the police service as well as we might. I believe that it is only by letting the public know what we do that the service will get the support it needs. I was pleased when the Police College at Bramshill opened its doors to the public; judging by the number of people who attended, there was obvious interest in what the police service was offering.

School children were shown around police stations and police officers visited schools to assist with road safety lectures. We also got more involved in careers conventions, all of which were positive ways in which 'to dress our shop window'. Many police officers helped with youth schemes, scouting, adventure groups, village fetes, old people's welfare or worked with the disabled, and most of this took place in their own time.

In my mind, I always wanted to see the police service develop not solely concentrating on law enforcement as the only focus, but rather in a more diversified role as a friend, counsellor, advisor, preventer and detector of crime.

Since my retirement, people have asked me what sort of advice I gave to new women police officers who were looking to make the most of their career and push the boundaries of their own individual goals. In many respects, I have always tried to answer in a way which reflected the route I took and how I approached life as a career member of the police force. It is probably best summed up in a talk I used to deliver, as a member of the Home Office team in the late 1970s, to groups of female police officers just starting their initial training course. It was a way of trying to welcome them into a unique industry and encourage them to have a clear and open mind. It went something like this:

You have all taken a major decision in your lives – a decision to become a policewoman. Having taken it, you are beginning to find out some of the things a police officer is required to know before starting out on the job.

You now belong to a rather select group of women. There are still only 8,500 policewomen in the country – one of the smallest numbers in any profession, trade or job. Be proud of your office, carry your heads high and when the public look at you – and they will, because you are a rare sight – be determined that your uniform is the smartest they will ever see. Your force and, indeed, the whole police service will be judged on you, the individual.

Make your minds up here and now at this training centre that you are going to give a service second to none. Anyone can be a mediocre, run-of-the-mill individual, but it requires so much more to be a good policewoman. Learn as much as you can, for knowledge is power; not only from books, but from your force orders, from your colleagues and from your supervisory officers. We are, all of us, no matter what our rank, constantly learning throughout our service. By wanting to do a good job, by being willing to learn, including from mistakes, willing to ask and showing enthusiasm, each one of you can be the policewoman chosen for the special jobs, the one always requested by name because you have gained a reputation for your thoroughness, willingness and adaptability. The officer in the CID will say, 'Can I have Miss X for special observation duty or for a special enquiry?'. Unfortunately, I have known officers make such a request and if the policewoman they ask for is not available, they prefer to leave the enquiry until she is – this reflects rather badly upon the other members of the department.

Life in the police service, particularly for a woman, can be interesting and all-absorbing. You get out of the job just what you put in; if you put in nothing, that is exactly what you will get out of it.

Some of the work will be fairly routine, but early, very early, in your service you will become involved in enquiries of a very serious nature for no other reason than that you are a woman. You may be on the fringe of a murder enquiry; you may take the statement from a complainant regarding an allegation of rape or a serious assault. At the other end of the scale, you may try to console a scruffy, runny-nosed, lost three-year-old who doesn't want your chocolate drops or ice cream or anything else to do with you and merely wants to scream his head off for as long as he can keep it up. Give to all these jobs your best – taking everything as it comes – and you will go a long way to maintaining the good name of the policewomen in your force.

The good reputation of women police has taken years to build up – something over 50 years – by women who have surmounted many trials and tribulations and who have overcome much male prejudice during that time. This heritage has been handed down to us to preserve and build upon.

I would recommend to all of you now, at this stage of your service, to set your sights on a goal for the future and to take steps to achieve that goal. As soon as you complete your probationary period – two years – you will be eligible to take the promotion examination. This examination is held once a year – for constables in November and for sergeants in January.

There is the special course at the Police College to be thought of – an accelerated promotion scheme. If you pass the many hurdles and are accepted for this course, you become a temporary sergeant immediately. On successfully completing one year, you return to your force a substantive sergeant; you are exempted from taking the examination to become an inspector and instead become one after a further years' service. This means you may become an inspector with less than five years' service. Of course, holding such a rank carries with it many responsibilities: you have to make decisions on the spot; you are capable of working on your own initiative.

The changing role of women in society today (1970s) means that most will work for a salary during their lives, even after marriage. So why not plan to stay on in this service after marriage? It is very noticeable when visiting forces today that a high proportion of the complement is married. This applies to all ranks from the Commander in charge of the Metropolitan women police to constable – married to policemen or to civilians. It is not an easy task to hold a very responsible job, run a home and look after a husband: but many women have made the most of the opportunities presented to them.

So far, I have managed to get you through the promotion examinations, through the special course and promoted to inspector and even to have some of you married in the process! There is another scheme which I have not mentioned. That is the possibility of obtaining a Bramshill Scholarship – Bramshill being the name of the Police College as you know – this scheme is open to members of the special course and the inspector's course. Various chief inspectors in charge of women police at forces around the country have obtained their BSc. through this scheme.

Even though the majority will not have the advantage of this further formal education, the contribution each one of you makes will be of equal, though different, importance. We all possess various skills and talents and we should each use these to the best advantage. Those who try to do as little as possible – the uniform carriers – are merely inadequate and should be pitied: they lose so much of life and of living. There is room in the police service for such a wide variety of talents, for we are dealing every day with every type of person across every age group.

The past work of women in this service, their ideals, their energies and their foresight contributed to ensuring that women are today employed in every branch of the service. Decide what your contribution is going to be – what will those who join in 10 years' time say of you? That you widened the horizon even further or that ground has been lost – for we cannot stand still, we either go forward or we slip back.

I know what I want to feel in years to come: to be bursting with pride at the roles taken and achievements made by women from across the police service, having confronted the challenges of a changing society, and achieved social equality with an unparalleled determination and passion to succeed.

And now, 40 years into my retirement, I can reflect on those achievements and the change which has taken place. It really is a remarkable change: a complete transformation in fact. Looking way back to the start of the Second World War there were 182 different police forces, made up of the Metropolitan force, the City of London force, 58 county forces and 122 forces from patrolling cities and boroughs. Over the years, this has been successfully streamlined to 43 separate provincial forces through the various amalgamations and restructuring processes, thereby allowing for much greater efficiencies and more consistent professional methods of policing around the country.

Has the role of women in the police force intensified over the last 70 years or so? Well, looking first at the number of officers across the police force, just prior to the start of the war in 1939, there were around 60,000 officers of which only 246 were women, representing less than 0.3% of the police workforce. If we move forward to the end of March 2019, the Office for National Office indicated that there were over 123,000 officers. Of this figure, nearly 37,500 were female officers: around 30% of the total.

This is a remarkable increase. Miss de Vitré and her pioneering predecessors paved the way, whilst my generation continued the push by making the women PC's role an essential part of the Service. From 1976 the Sex Discrimination Act opened the doors for a new generation of women to look at the police service as a genuine career opportunity. Hindsight is a wonderful thing, and with this in mind, I admit I was wrong about the effects of the Sex Discrimination Act. I did not feel that the police service should be incorporated but these figures say otherwise. Women have been able to progress, with many having subsequently reached the highest ranks across the range of departments. This simply would not have been possible had the service been excluded from the Act.

How times change. I feel incredibly privileged and grateful to have enjoyed such a fulfilling career spanning 30 years. During this time, I can honestly say that I worked with the same enthusiasm, commitment and determination from the very first day I walked into the station at Richmond, to the day I left employment at the Home Office in London. The challenges may have been many and varied and at times very testing indeed, but work is always very much what you make of it and I can proudly say that I made my police work my life across those three decades of employment.

The payback has been enormous. My career has enabled me to enjoy 40 years of retirement (and counting), during which I have been able to draw on my vast experiences gained in the police force to great effect in everyday normal civilian life. I feel utterly contented.

CHAPTER 11

RETIREMENT – LIFE AFTER THE POLICE

Sitting here as I do now, having just celebrated my 90th birth-day, I can look back with total contentment on 40 years of retirement and, more specifically, back to 1979 when a key chapter of my life closed. My 30-year career in the police force had come to an end, and I had achieved far more than I had anticipated when I first set foot on the beat. I had no real plans for what to do next…

Most senior police officers who retired at my age moved on to do something completely different on a new career path, normally in some sort of corporate industry where, with their experience, they could adapt to a different sort of structured working life. Quite simply, I didn't want to do that. I felt I had done my bit, working hard and building my career in the police force by serving the public to the best of my ability. There was no other industry in which I wanted to work, so I ultimately came to an easy decision, and one which I have never regretted. I gave up work, safe in the full knowledge that my police pension would see me through for the rest of my life. However, I didn't want to sit back and do nothing so I made it my goal to try to continue giving service to the public, whenever and wherever I could. This time it would be in a voluntary capacity through getting involved in different organisations.

My first major decision was to choose where my retirement home would take roots. The time I had spent with my sister and her family made it an easier decision than I had first thought. May was my only sister and whilst working at the Home Office, I had got used to spending quality time with her and her husband, Brian, along with their three children, Jen, Wendy and Tony. It was becoming too much of a wrench to leave, after spending the last few years in their company and getting to know them all so well. My mother was still living in the north-east, but that was easily solved as she moved south to take up residence in May's home. Meanwhile, I sold my house in Northumberland and bought a new property in Maidenhead, only a short distance away from my sister's house.

I felt as though I could easily settle in the south of England after so much travelling and moving around the country, visiting stations and living in a variety of rented accommodation. I had become very familiar with Berkshire during my time at the Home Office and it felt as though I belonged here. I had made myself a secondary home through attending church at St Luke's and quickly got to know many locals, including several who have become my closest companions and true friends. Within a month or so of retiring, the vicar asked me to become church-warden, which meant I was able to get much more actively involved in the parish itself and the community at large. Oddly, at the time I was the only woman warden in the deanery, and I felt a little haunted that my early years as a female police officer were being re-enacted in civilian life as a solitary woman in a man's world! Thankfully, this proved not to be the case and in the years following my retirement, it has been refreshing to see women flourish alongside men in their careers across a whole plethora of different industries.

My influence at church led to new doors being opened and it wasn't very long before I became a school governor at the church primary school, before being elected chair of governors in the years which followed. The school governing body was instrumental in setting out the school's vision, mitigating financial risk and scrutinising educational matters. As you would expect, I took my role as a school governor seriously, especially as I had seen many very young and early teenage children suffer during the course of my police responsibilities. In some small way, this new role gave me the opportunity to carry on fighting for the innocent, but in a completely different capacity.

Our team of governors were exactly that… a team working together, ensuring that the school provided a good-quality education for all pupils, whilst trying to raise standards of achievement every year. I found it very therapeutic to get more closely involved in the school community, working alongside the headteacher and senior leaders in the town. Perhaps it was also, in some small way, cathartic for me after dealing with so many distressing cases of non-accidental injuries to children.

My role in church affairs developed further and it wasn't long before I was an elected member of the Deanery Synod, followed by the Diocesan Synod. These connected me to the local network of churches in the area, in efforts to inspire, influence and lead mission and ministry. The Deanery Synod consisted of lay members, elected every third year at annual parochial church meetings, together with the clergy of the deanery (a group of parishes). We were a body which reflected on issues of concern to the church and the community at a local level within the Windsor and Maidenhead area.

On a broader scale, each diocese was under the jurisdiction of a bishop and each Diocesan Synod consisted of the bishop, clergy and elected laity, of which I was one. Our mission was to consider matters sent from the General Synod (the national assembly of the Church of England) and from deaneries, formulating diocesan policy on a wide range of issues, advising the bishop as appropriate and taking votes on various aspects of administration. I was very familiar with the emphasis behind helping and serving a community, whilst approaching topics of a more strategic nature were very fresh in my mind from my latter days of working at the Home Office.

Pastoral work of this nature was of great interest to me and also brought great satisfaction, knowing that I was continuing my efforts to serve the public. My attachment to the community continued to grow and I took pleasure in getting involved in simple but very worthwhile tasks, like delivering meals on wheels to the needy, holding coffee mornings at church functions, and editing and reading the *Talking Newspaper* for the blind.

The church has been 'my rock' throughout retirement, and to this day, much of what I do in life revolves around functions and activities associated with St Luke's and my circle of friends who attend the church. Going back to the 1980s and around the time that many Vietnamese refugees were escaping their war-torn country, the UK received an influx of immigrants who became known as the Vietnamese Boat People. One of the decisions made by the church was to take responsibility for a house allocated by the council in which a Vietnamese family could be housed. Our parishioners were so supportive and generous with their monetary donations and help to clean and furnish the house in readiness for the family. We were thrilled to have welcomed the lovely family who were able to settle in our town and call it their new home. I still keep in touch with their daughter to this day. Sadly, the parents have both died but their daughter is still living in the house which she subsequently bought. She is now married and has worked continuously since coming to the UK all those years ago.

In a similar vein, back in February 1993, following a Churches Together meeting, it was suggested that we considered the feasibility of opening a Child Contact Centre in Maidenhead. I was part of the planning group which discussed this option, and after considerable research and taking professional advice, we managed to open the Centre in Maidenhead, based at the United Reformed Church, during September of that year. My involvement with broken families during my police career and seeing the negative impact this had on children gave me the impetus to fight hard and get the centre agreed and then established.

Effectively the Maidenhead Child Contact Centre was and still is, a place where the children of separated families can enjoy contact with one or both parents and sometimes other family members in a relaxed, safe and neutral environment. It was created as an accredited voluntary organisation which opens twice a month with no charge for the service provided. It proved to be a really promising venture and I'm pleased to say the centre is valued as much today as it was when it opened 26 years ago.

Many families have benefitted over the years and as a result we expanded by opening another centre in neighbouring Slough, which was administered and supported by the local Soroptimist Club and is still used today. Each centre provides a service which helps estranged families, but most significantly the children, who suffer as a result of the breakdown through no fault of their own. I feel warmly contented that I have helped in some small way to make these children's lives a little easier and more bearable, at a time when their domestic life may have been in turmoil. It has certainly achieved its objectives of allowing non-resident parents to have contact with their children in a relaxed and safe environment.

I've been a member of Soroptimist International for the last half century and it has been a central pillar of activity for me during my retirement years. In a nutshell, this is a worldwide service organisation for women, working for peace, and with a central focus to improve the lives of women and girls. All the work – local, national or international – generated through the Soroptimist group is linked to the United Nations Sustainable Development Goals. All projects work towards ending poverty, eradicating hunger, providing education for all and preserving the environment. As a result of attending regular meetings with my local group and others from around the UK, I have been able to keep in touch with local issues and been made aware of a wide range of international challenges. We've offered support as a group, helping with charity and fundraising events.

Meetings have been therapeutic and have given me the opportunity to talk to several different groups about my career in the police force, whilst at the same time, listen to stories from many brilliant women who have done some extraordinary things in their lives. It's all been a far cry from living in a man's world!

I have been able to enjoy time simply getting to know people, talking to different people from different backgrounds, in very much the same way I used to talk to civilians on my beat. Communicating in a simple, friendly and engaging manner should be the simplest of tasks and makes life so much easier for everyone. I guess it is an artform, but I wish more people in positions of power worked at it, because freedom to talk openly makes such a positive impression. I have made many friends from all walks of life by talking and getting to know them; some of my closest friends have come from within the police force, but I've also forged amazing friendships with people I have met through church and social occasions.

I have enjoyed annual holidays with my close friend Joan Harnby for the last 20 or so years, venturing around Europe and the British Isles, generally relaxing with a good book but never too far away from a pot of tea and delicious homemade cake and scones! Joan and her late husband, Gordon, both grew up in the north-east in and around Middlesbrough, so could easily identify with the areas where I had worked whilst they were still living there. It is entirely possible we could have even met unknowingly at some point back in the sixties whilst I was doing my rounds – strange thought! In the summer of 2019, we holidayed on the Northumberland coastline close to the charming Holy Island of Lindisfarne. It was strange going back to my old neck of the woods where I had spent so many wonderful years working, but a thrill to once again enjoy the beautiful scenery which that part of the country offers. I felt very much at peace that I had done my bit and was fully at ease to be back there in civilian clothes enjoying all the hospitality on offer.

Undoubtedly, the activities which I have undertaken during retirement would not have been possible for me had I not gained the experiences within my police career. My years in the force gave me strength, perseverance and a confidence which would have been impossible to gain in any other walk of life and for that I am truly grateful.

I have been blessed with good health, a supportive family and great friends and without all of those in abundance, I simply could not have achieved what I did. The same is true of my faith: it really was a rock to me in times of stress and when faced with challenging and harrowing cases, involving the innocent, and the vulnerable. There were times when I did feel isolated particularly in my senior positions when there was no one to turn to. That saying, 'It's lonely at the top' was on occasions reality for me. I am forever thankful that God has been there whenever I have called upon Him.

It had never been my intention to set about recording my memoirs, but as the decades have gone by, I have realised that the world has changed so much through the technical revolution and a social transformation, and I didn't want the efforts that were undertaken by me and my colleagues to be lost in the mists of time. Please forgive me if some of my memories may be a little patchy, but I am relying on my 90-year-old brain to recall a career which started over 70 years ago. I hope you enjoyed reading them.

Royal Almonry Office
Buckingham Palace
London SW1A 1AA

020 7930 4832

18th November, 2019

Dear Miss Sigsworth,

The Royal Maundy Service

On Thursday, 9th April, 2020, The Queen will attend the Royal Maundy Service in St. George's Chapel, Windsor Castle at 11.00 a.m. during which Her Majesty will distribute Maundy gifts of specially minted coins to the Maundy Recipients. This year the Maundy Recipients have been chosen from across the United Kingdom. The precise number of Recipients is equal to The Queen's age and on this occasion there will be 94 men and 94 women chosen to attend the Royal Maundy Service. I am delighted to inform you that your name has been submitted by the Bishop of your Diocese to be one of the Maundy Recipients and I very much hope that you will feel able to accept this honour.

Each Recipient is invited to bring one Companion to accompany them on Maundy Thursday. Your Companion should be able to look after you on the day and ideally would be a spouse/partner, family member or close friend who will sit next to you in the Chapel.

Further details will be sent to you in the New Year once you have returned the completed form to us. Your Diocesan Bishop's Office will also be in touch with you to offer advice on accommodation and planning your journey to and from Windsor for the Royal Maundy Service.

We look forward to receiving your completed form by Friday, 17th January and hope that you will be able to accept this invitation.

Yours sincerely,

Paul Leddington Wright,
Secretary, Royal Almonry

In November 2019 I was excited to have received a letter from Buckingham Palace informing me I was invited to the Royal Maundy Service at St George's Chapel, Windsor, where I would be a recipient of the Maundy Gift. Little did I know then that my excitement would change to huge disappointment because of the outbreak of Covid 19 in the spring of 2020.

April, 2020

Dear Miss Sigsworth,

I have great pleasure in sending you the Maundy Gift which, unfortunately, I am unable to distribute to you personally at the Royal Maundy Service in St. George's Chapel, Windsor Castle, on Thursday, 9th April. This ancient Christian ceremony, which reflects Jesus's instruction to his Disciples to love one another, is a call to the service of others, something that has been at the centre of my life. I believe it is a call to service for all of us.

It is one of my most rewarding duties as Sovereign to observe this highly significant ceremony at such an important point in the Christian calendar. I know that you, as a Recipient of this year's Maundy Gift, will be as deeply disappointed as I am that it is not going ahead, while understanding the necessary decision in the current circumstances.

However, this should not mean your invaluable contribution within the community goes unnoticed, and I am sending this Maundy Gift to thank you for your Christian service.

My thoughts and prayers are with you and your families at this difficult time.

With my best wishes to you this Easter.

Elizabeth R

Miss Phyllis Sigsworth

My precious letter I received from the Queen, following
the cancellation of the Royal Maundy Service to which I had
been invited. Its cancellation was due to the dreadful
coronavirus outbreak which affected us all in 2020.